LIBERTÉ
EGALITÉ
BEYONCÉ

LIBERTÉ
EGALITÉ
BEYONCÉ

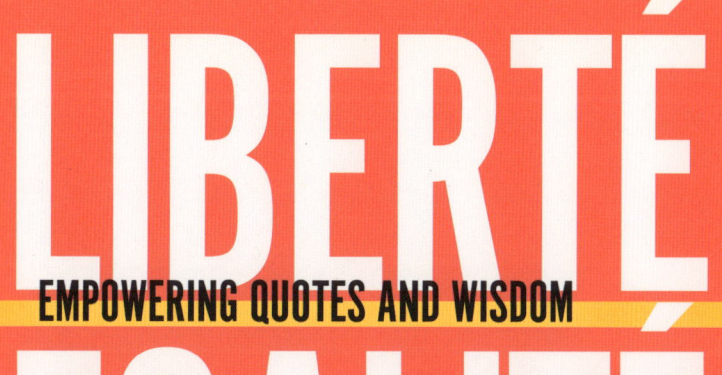

EMPOWERING QUOTES AND WISDOM

FROM OUR FIERCE AND FLAWLESS QUEEN

JOHN DAVIS

ILLUSTRATIONS BY ELIZA WILSON

Smith Street Books

CONTENTS

DESTINY 8

THE PHENOMENON 26

QUEEN BEY 58

GODDESS 88

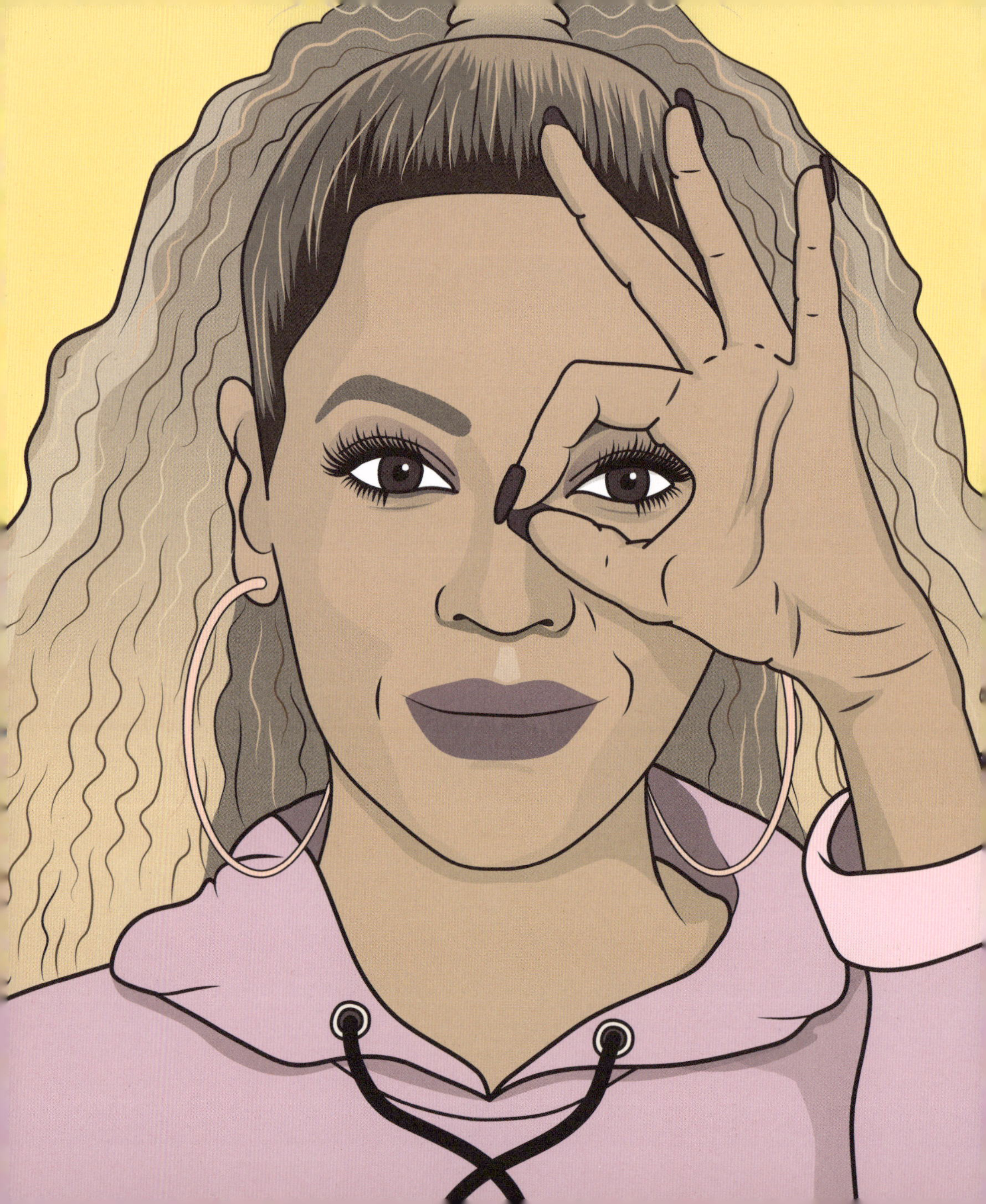

Beyoncé Knowles-Carter is all things: jaw-droppingly talented, breathtakingly beautiful, boundlessly successful.

Pop star, queen, musician, goddess, inspiration, activist, business mogul, feminist, mother, brand, cultural phenomenon, wife, artist, warrior, sister, icon.

She has no peer.

All hail Queen Bey.

DES

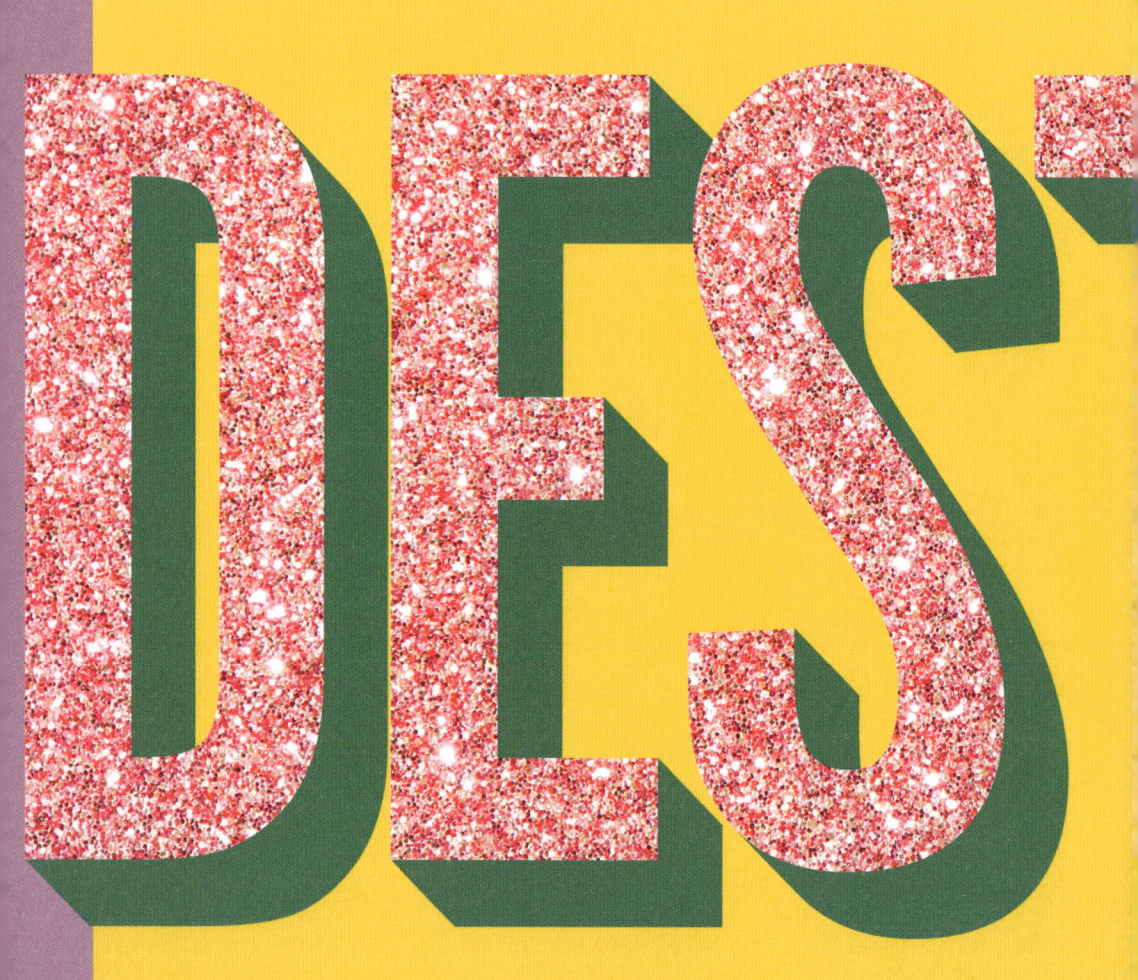

TINY

THE EARLY DAYS

Beyoncé Giselle Knowles-Carter was born in 1981 in Houston, Texas, to Mathew and Celestine 'Tina' Knowles.

Bey's name is a reference to her mother's maiden name, Beyincé.

Bey began her rise to superstardom in the early 90s in Girl's Tyme, a group which would eventually morph into Destiny's Child. Signed to Columbia Records in 1997 with their original line-up of Beyoncé, Kelly Rowland, LaTavia Roberson and LeToya Luckett – and with Bey's father, Mathew, as manager – Destiny's Child would go on to become one of the best-selling girl groups in history. Despite their success, the group was plagued with internal conflicts and line-up changes. The best-known and most successful version of the group featured Bey, Kelly Rowland and Michelle Williams – and while their friendships have had plenty of bumps over they years, there was no denying that the world collectively lost its mind when they reunited to tear up the stage during Beyoncé's 2018's Coachella set.

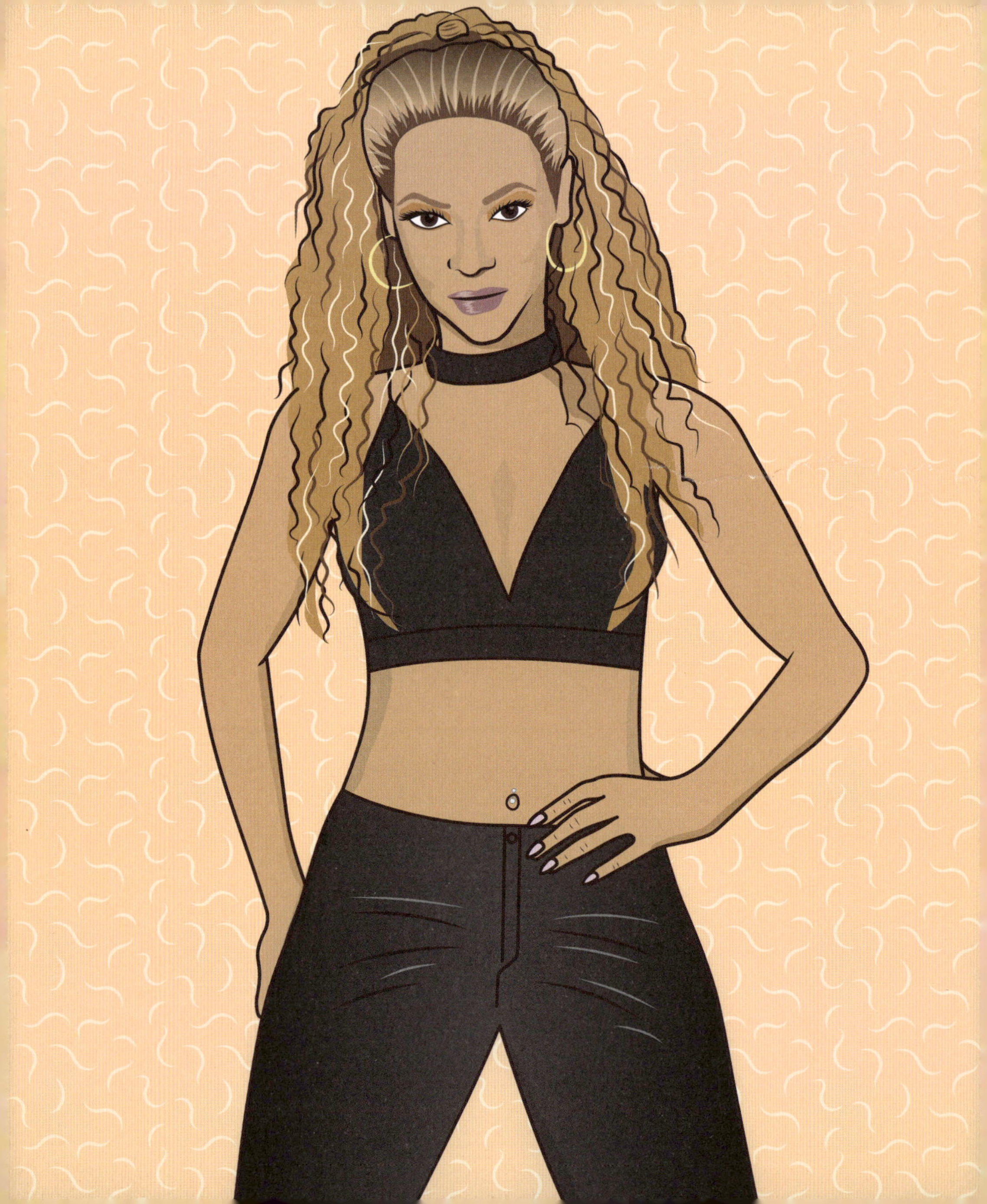

"We would like to be remembered as true friends. This is a group we love. And we love what we do and love doing that with each other. We'd like to be remembered for trying to empower other women, and for great music. Destiny's Child was founded on family, loyalty, and sisterhood and we love music, and we just want to share our gifts and our blessings with the world."

Michelle Williams

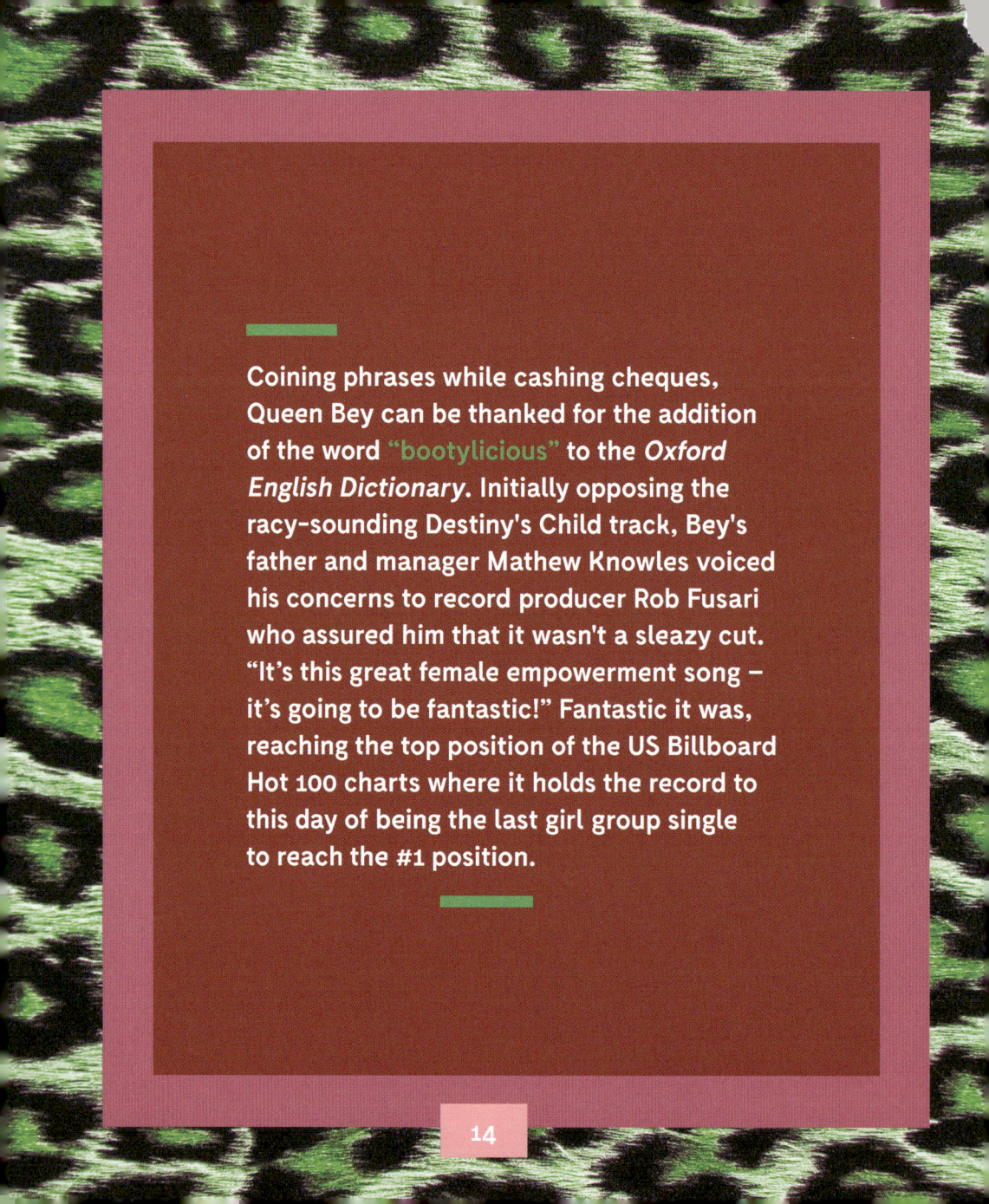

Coining phrases while cashing cheques, Queen Bey can be thanked for the addition of the word "bootylicious" to the *Oxford English Dictionary*. Initially opposing the racy-sounding Destiny's Child track, Bey's father and manager Mathew Knowles voiced his concerns to record producer Rob Fusari who assured him that it wasn't a sleazy cut. "It's this great female empowerment song – it's going to be fantastic!" Fantastic it was, reaching the top position of the US Billboard Hot 100 charts where it holds the record to this day of being the last girl group single to reach the #1 position.

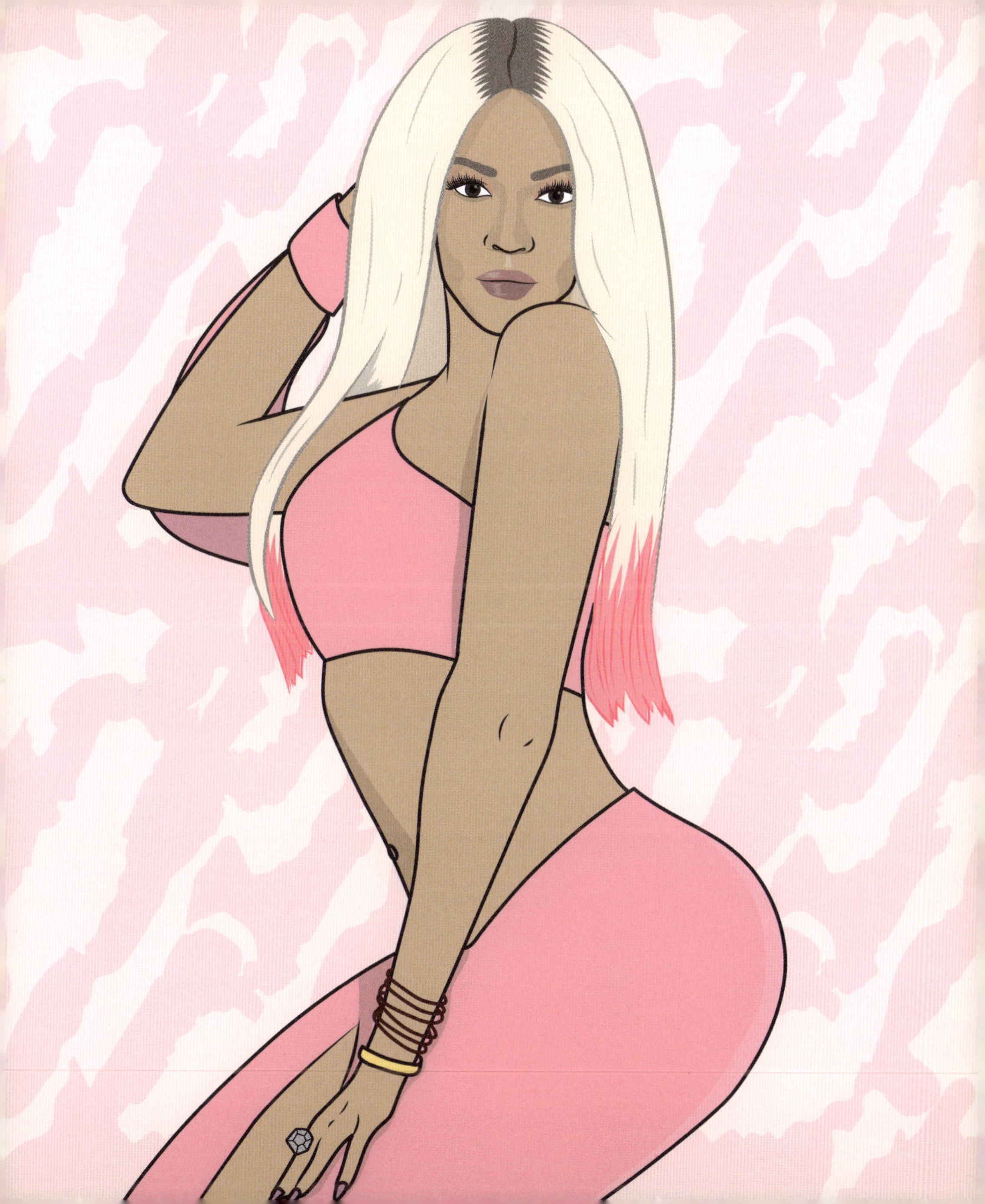

Before she was a 'Grown Woman' taking over the globe, Beyoncé won her first talent show at 7 years old. She received a standing ovation for her performance of John Lennon's world peace anthem 'Imagine'.

In her youth, Beyoncé would charge her parents and friends $5 each to watch her perform!

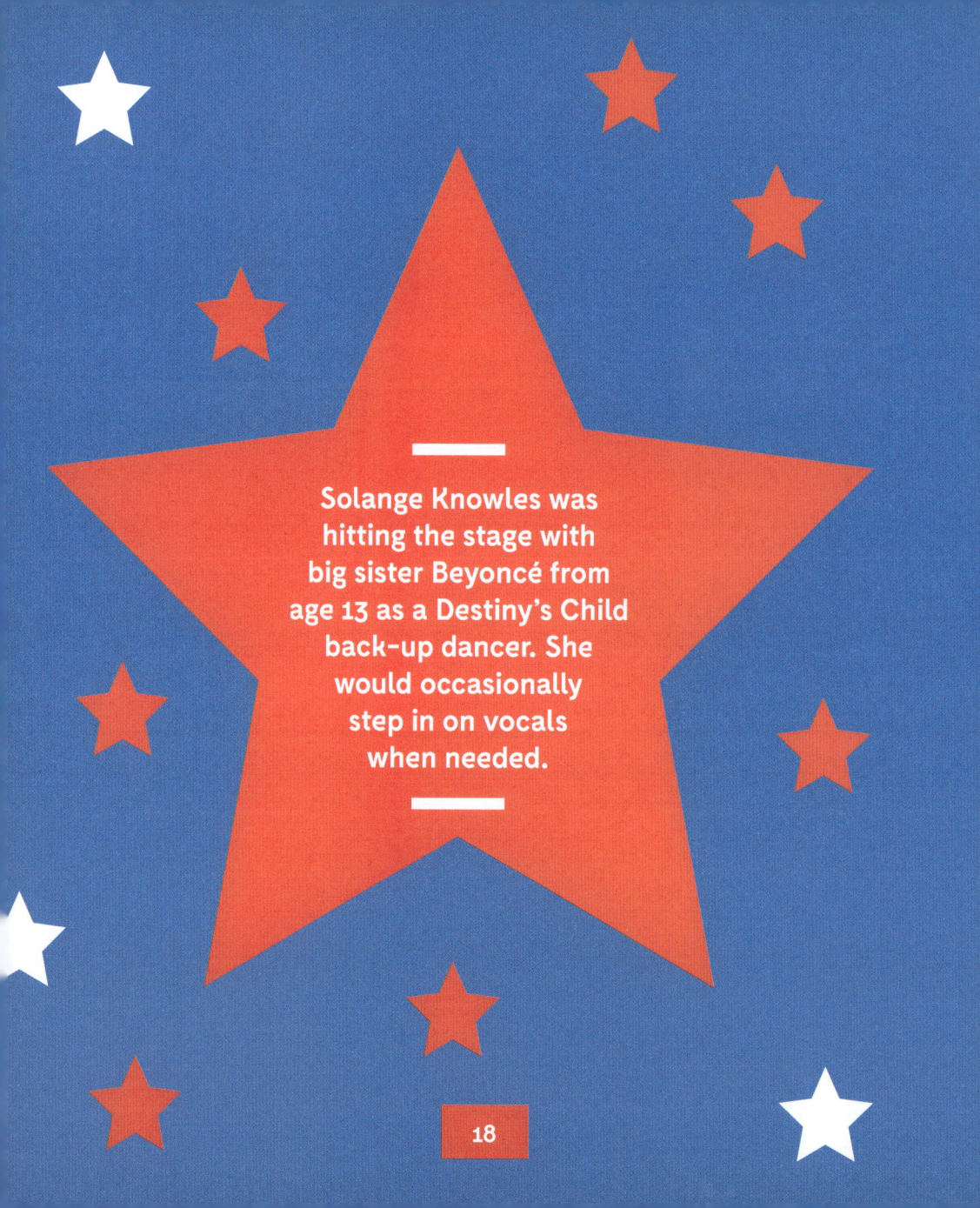

Solange Knowles was hitting the stage with big sister Beyoncé from age 13 as a Destiny's Child back-up dancer. She would occasionally step in on vocals when needed.

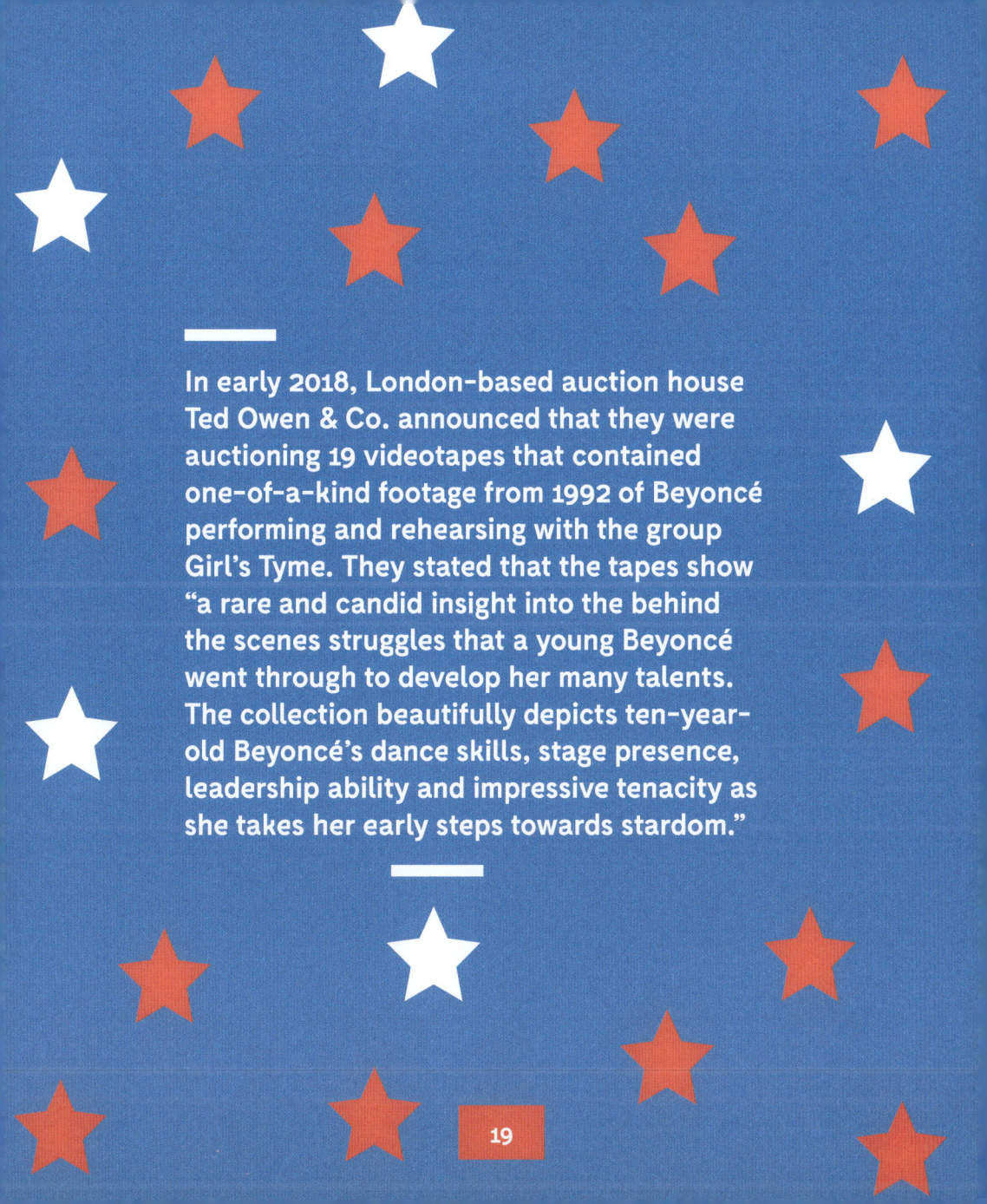

In early 2018, London-based auction house Ted Owen & Co. announced that they were auctioning 19 videotapes that contained one-of-a-kind footage from 1992 of Beyoncé performing and rehearsing with the group Girl's Tyme. They stated that the tapes show "a rare and candid insight into the behind the scenes struggles that a young Beyoncé went through to develop her many talents. The collection beautifully depicts ten-year-old Beyoncé's dance skills, stage presence, leadership ability and impressive tenacity as she takes her early steps towards stardom."

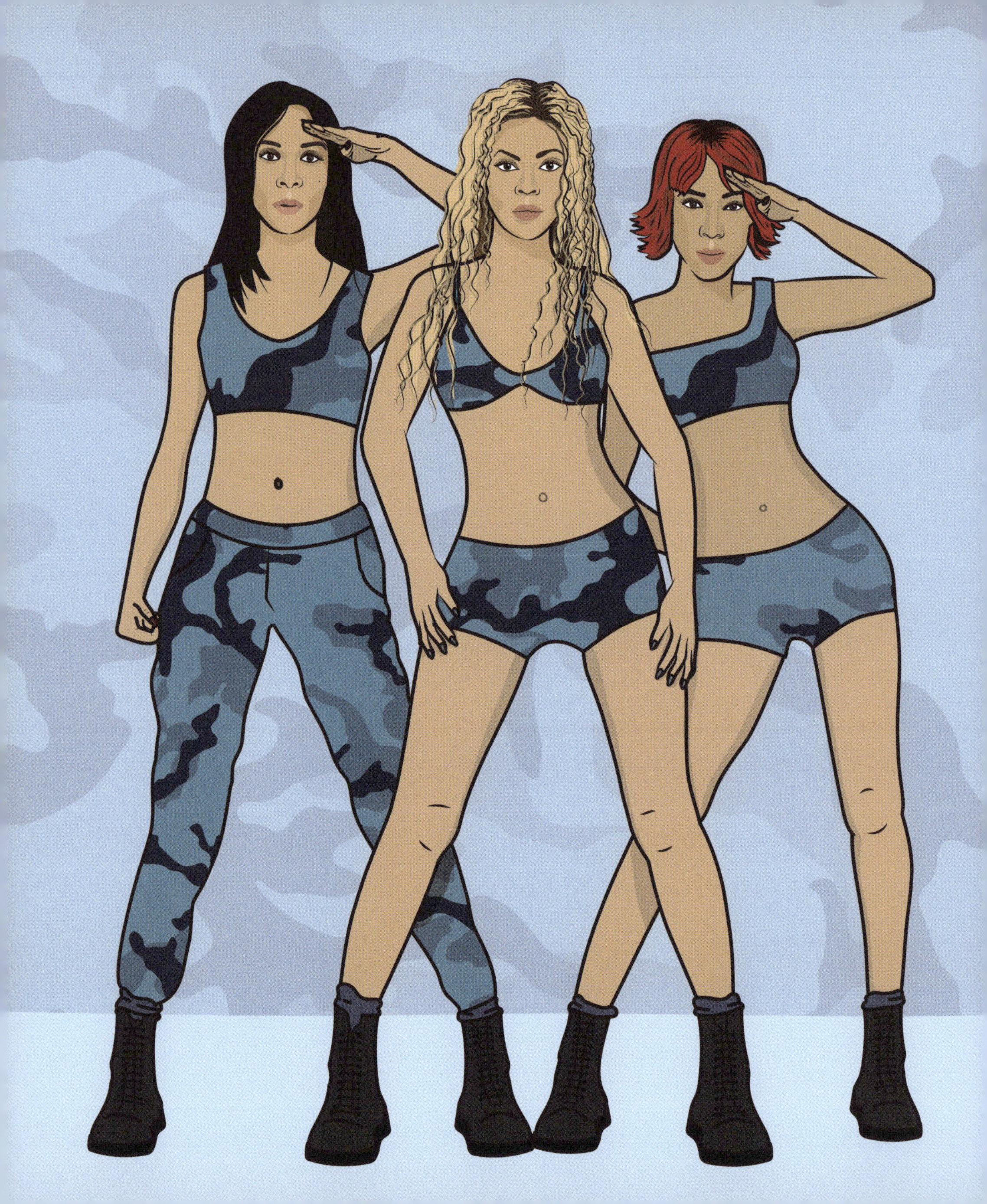

A timeless anthem for sisterhood and empowerment, 'Survivor' is Destiny's Child's message of endurance in the face of adversity. Beyoncé said in 2001, "The lyrics to 'Survivor' are Destiny's Child's story, because we've been through a lot. We went through our drama and everybody was like, 'Oh, well, no more Destiny's Child.' Well, we sold even more records after all of the changes. Any complications we've had in our ten-year period of time have made us closer and tighter and better."

TRIPLE THREAT TRIPLE THREAT

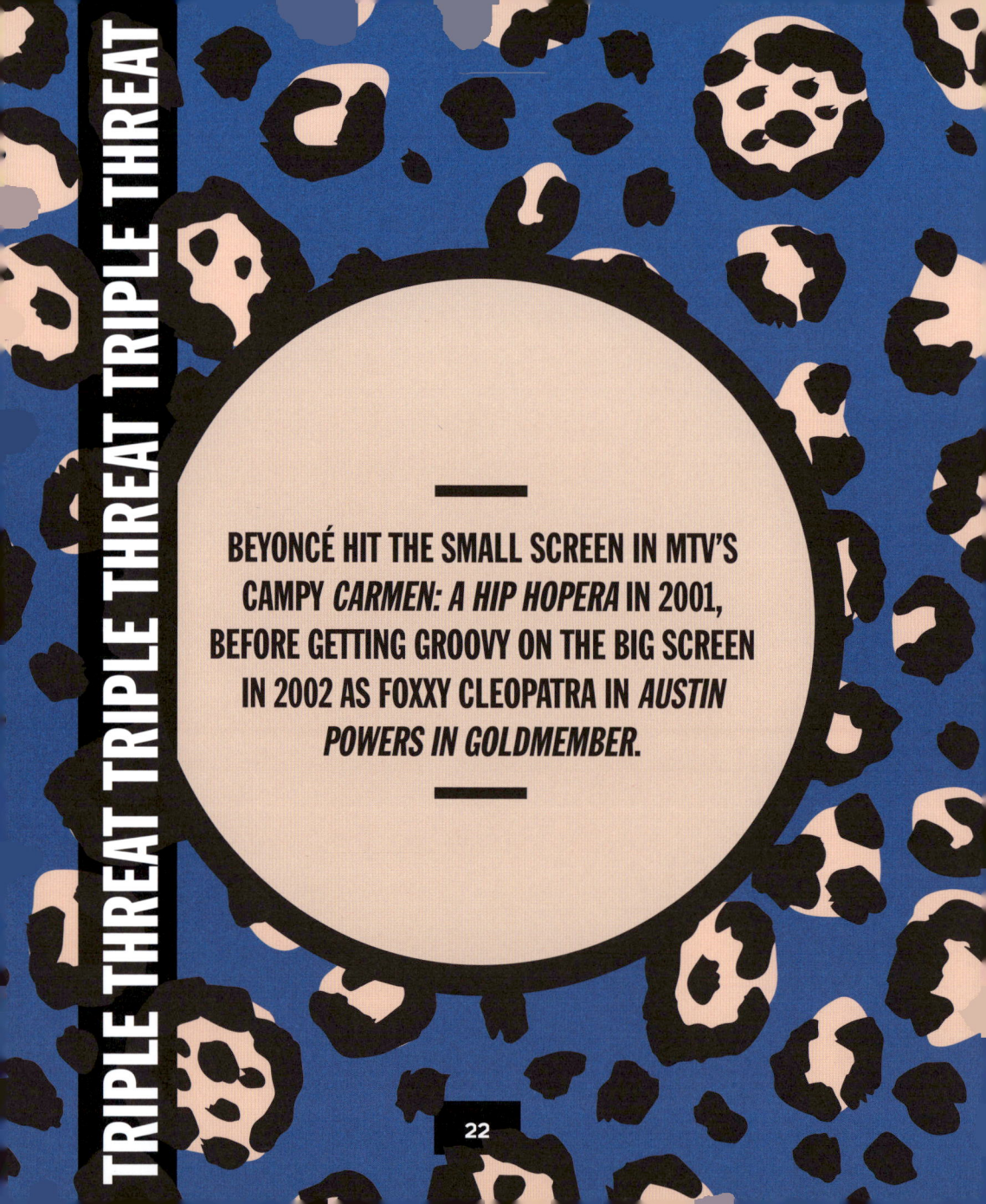

BEYONCÉ HIT THE SMALL SCREEN IN MTV'S CAMPY *CARMEN: A HIP HOPERA* IN 2001, BEFORE GETTING GROOVY ON THE BIG SCREEN IN 2002 AS FOXXY CLEOPATRA IN *AUSTIN POWERS IN GOLDMEMBER*.

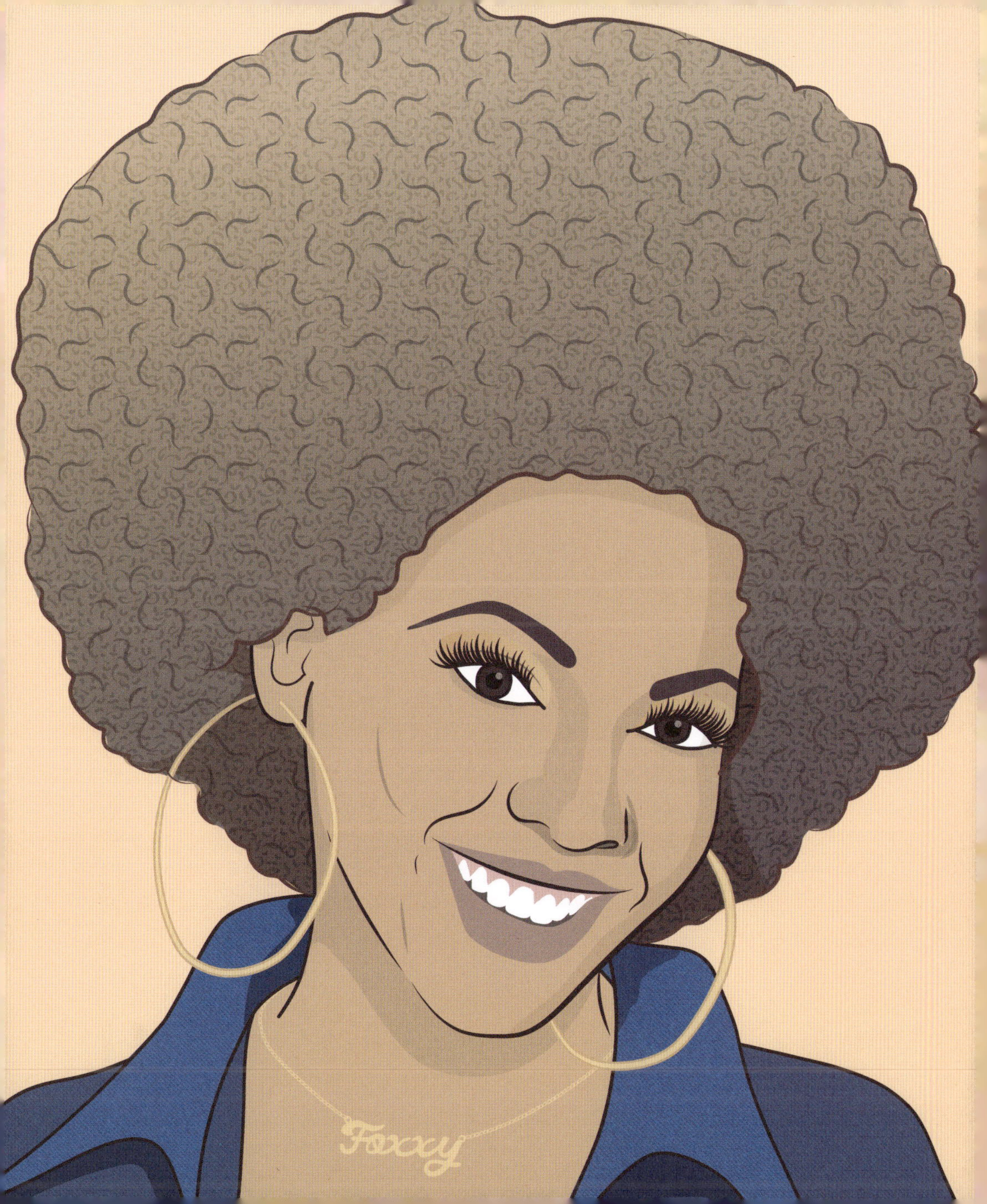
Foxxy

Beyoncé the solo artist descended on the world with *Dangerously in Love* in 2003. The album debuted at number one on the US Billboard chart — the first hint of the megastardom that would follow.

Despite her solo success, Beyoncé stayed with Destiny's Child. The group eventually announced their plans to split in 2005 and officially disbanded in 2006, following a farewell performance at an NBA All-Star Game in Houston, Texas.

Always one to come out of the gate strong, Bey's second solo album, *B'Day* – released to coincide with her 25th birthday – also debuted at number one and smashed her own previous record sales.

THE PHENO[M]

CHART CRUSHING

MENON

& RECORD BREAKING

As of November 2016, as a solo artist Beyoncé had sold over 26.1 million albums in the United States alone, and approximately 60 million albums worldwide. Throw in some cheeky additional Destiny's Child album sales – 18.6 million albums in the US and 40 million worldwide – and you have one of the best-selling recording artists of all time. She's the most nominated female artist in Grammy history, with 62 career nominations and 22 wins, not to mention the mountain of MTV VMAs, BET Awards, Soul Train Awards, American Music Awards and Billboard Music Awards she's won and been nominated for.

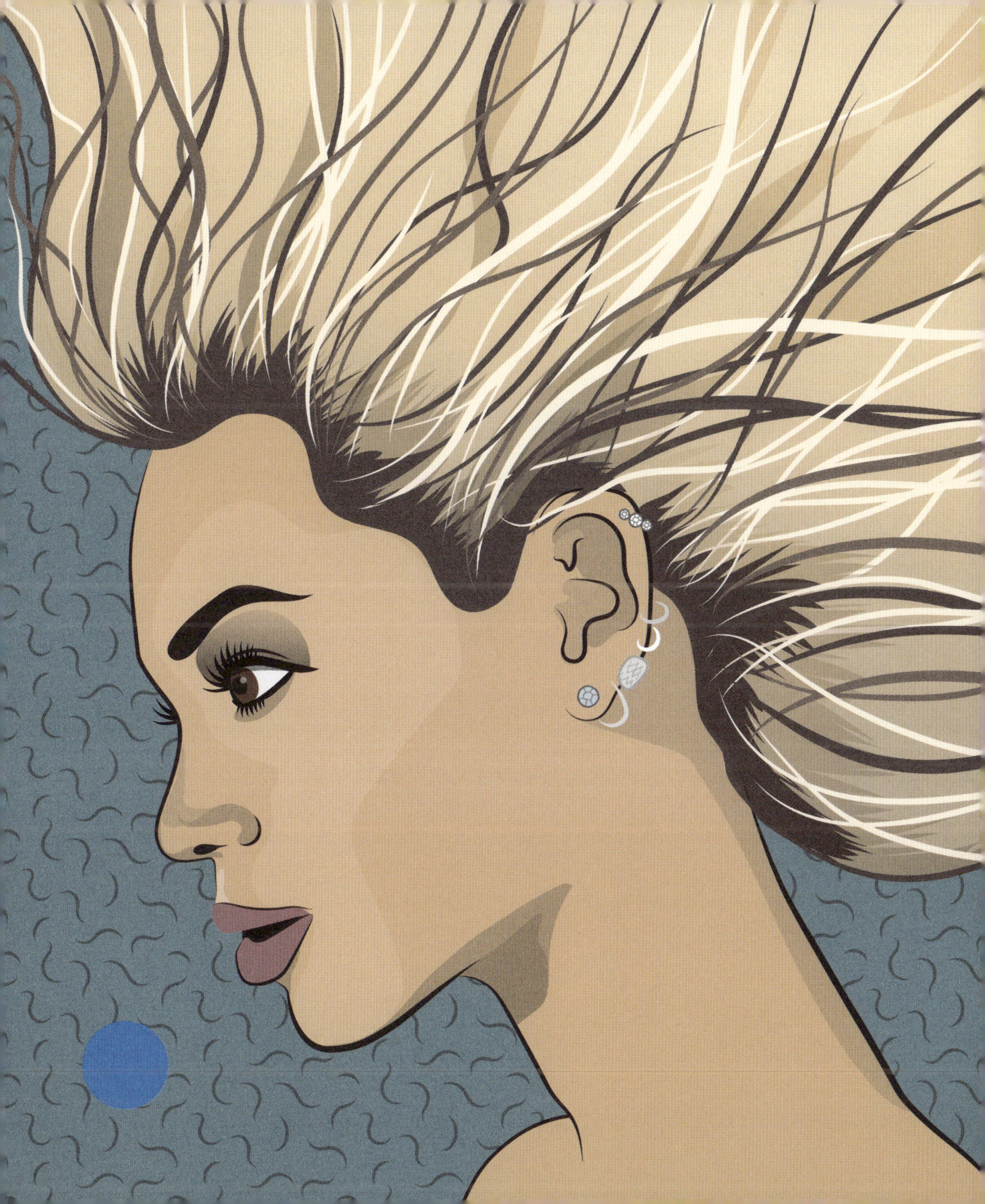

SOLO STUDIO ALBUMS

Dangerously in Love (2003)
US number 1, more than 16 million sold, 5 Grammy wins

B'Day (2006)
US number 1, more than 12 million sold, won the Grammy for Best Contemporary R&B Album

I Am… Sasha Fierce (2008)
US number 1, more than 16 million sold, 6 Grammy wins

4 (2011)
US number 1, more than 5 million sold, 1 Grammy win

Beyoncé (2013)
US number 1, more than 8 million sold, 3 Grammy wins

Lemonade (2016)
US number 1, more than 4 million sold, 2 Grammy wins

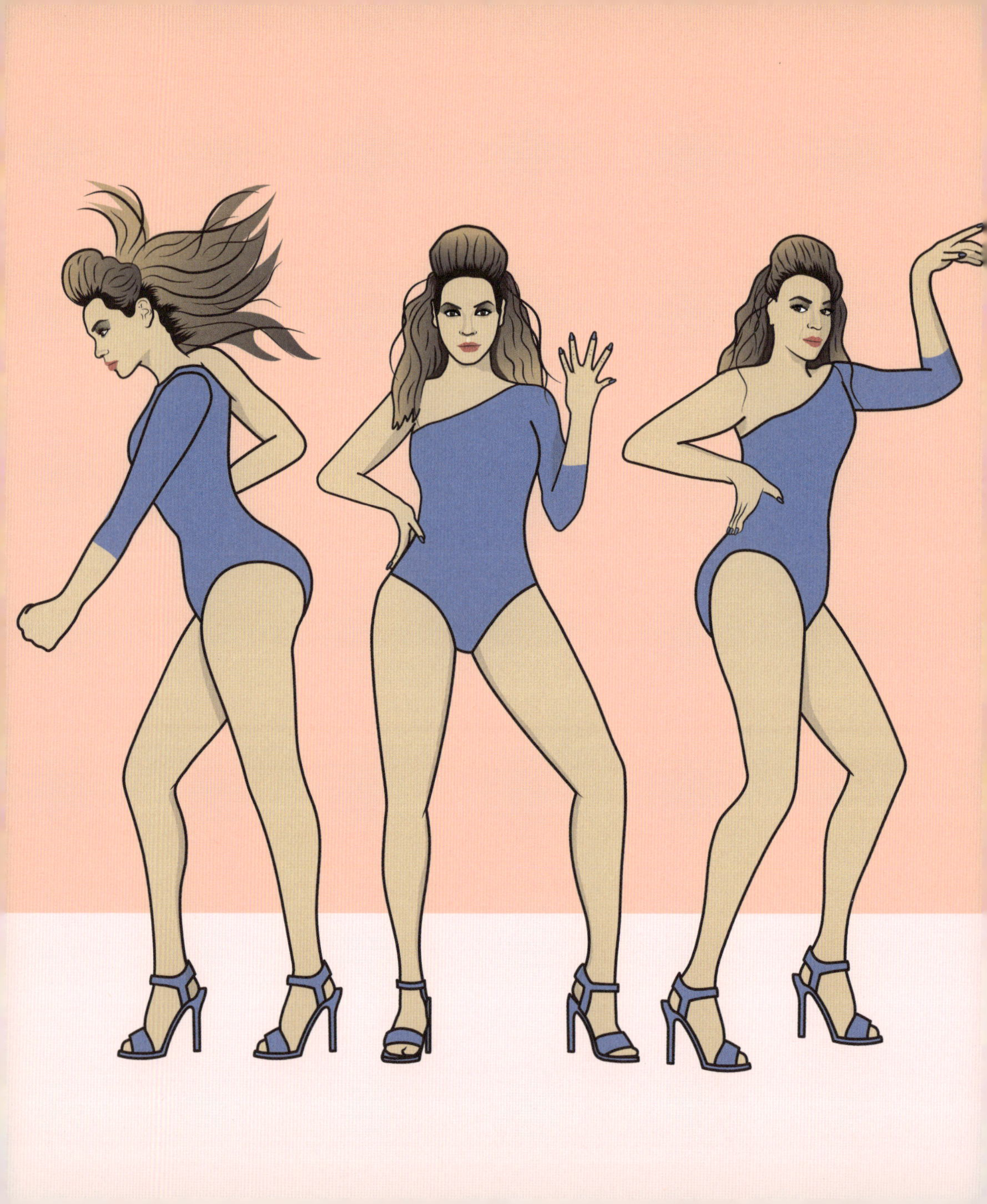

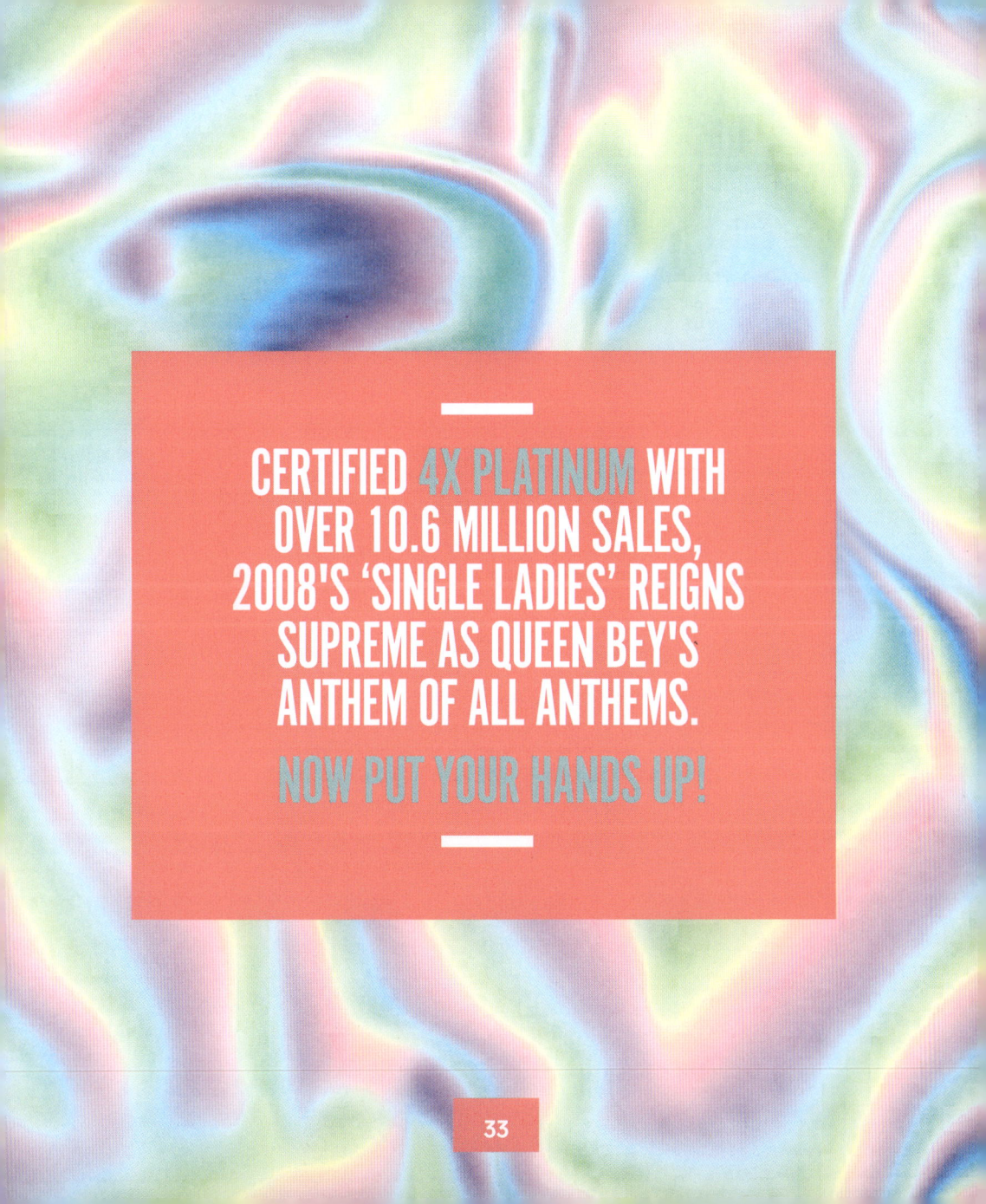

CERTIFIED 4X PLATINUM WITH OVER 10.6 MILLION SALES, 2008'S 'SINGLE LADIES' REIGNS SUPREME AS QUEEN BEY'S ANTHEM OF ALL ANTHEMS.

NOW PUT YOUR HANDS UP!

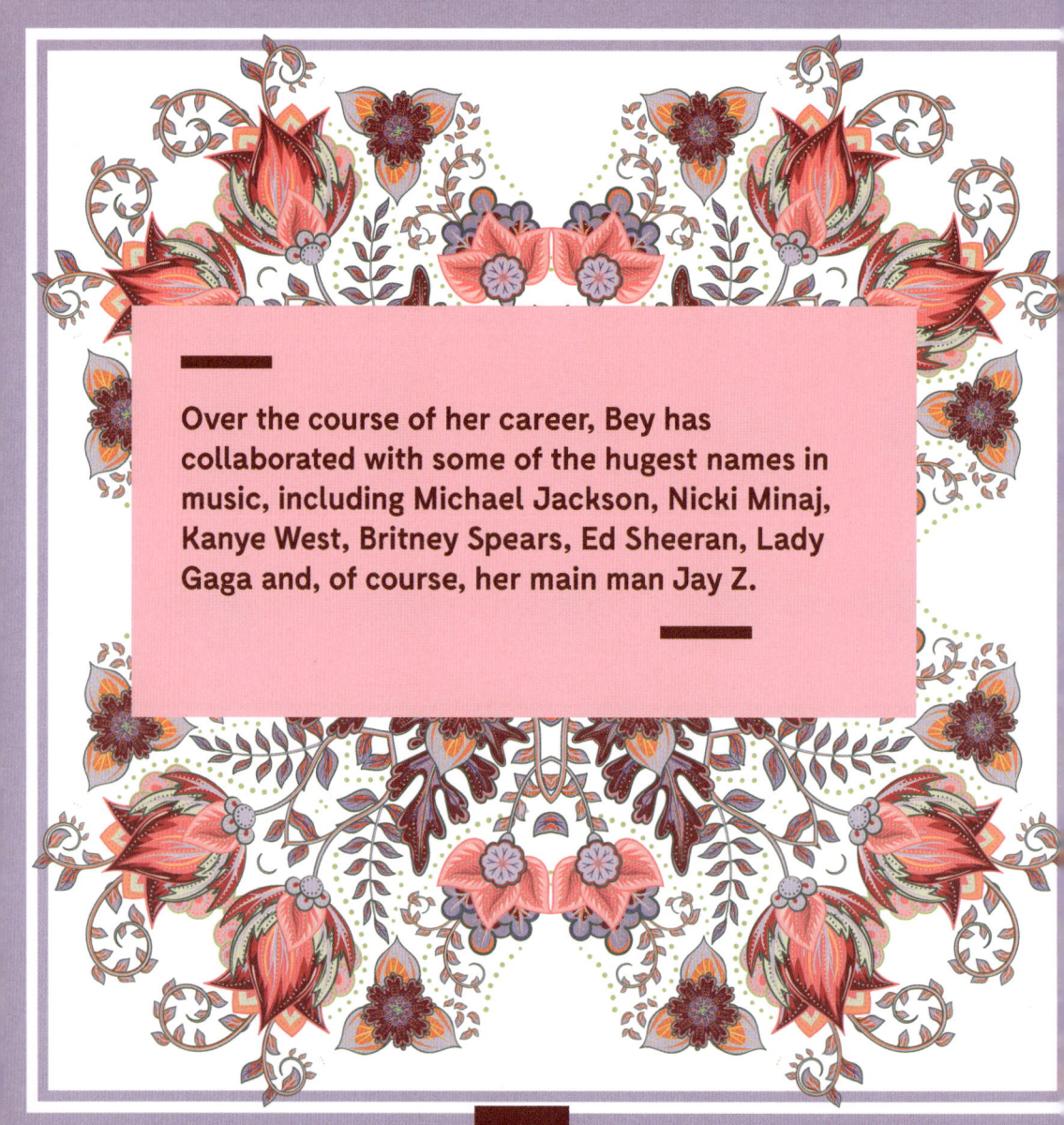

Over the course of her career, Bey has collaborated with some of the hugest names in music, including Michael Jackson, Nicki Minaj, Kanye West, Britney Spears, Ed Sheeran, Lady Gaga and, of course, her main man Jay Z.

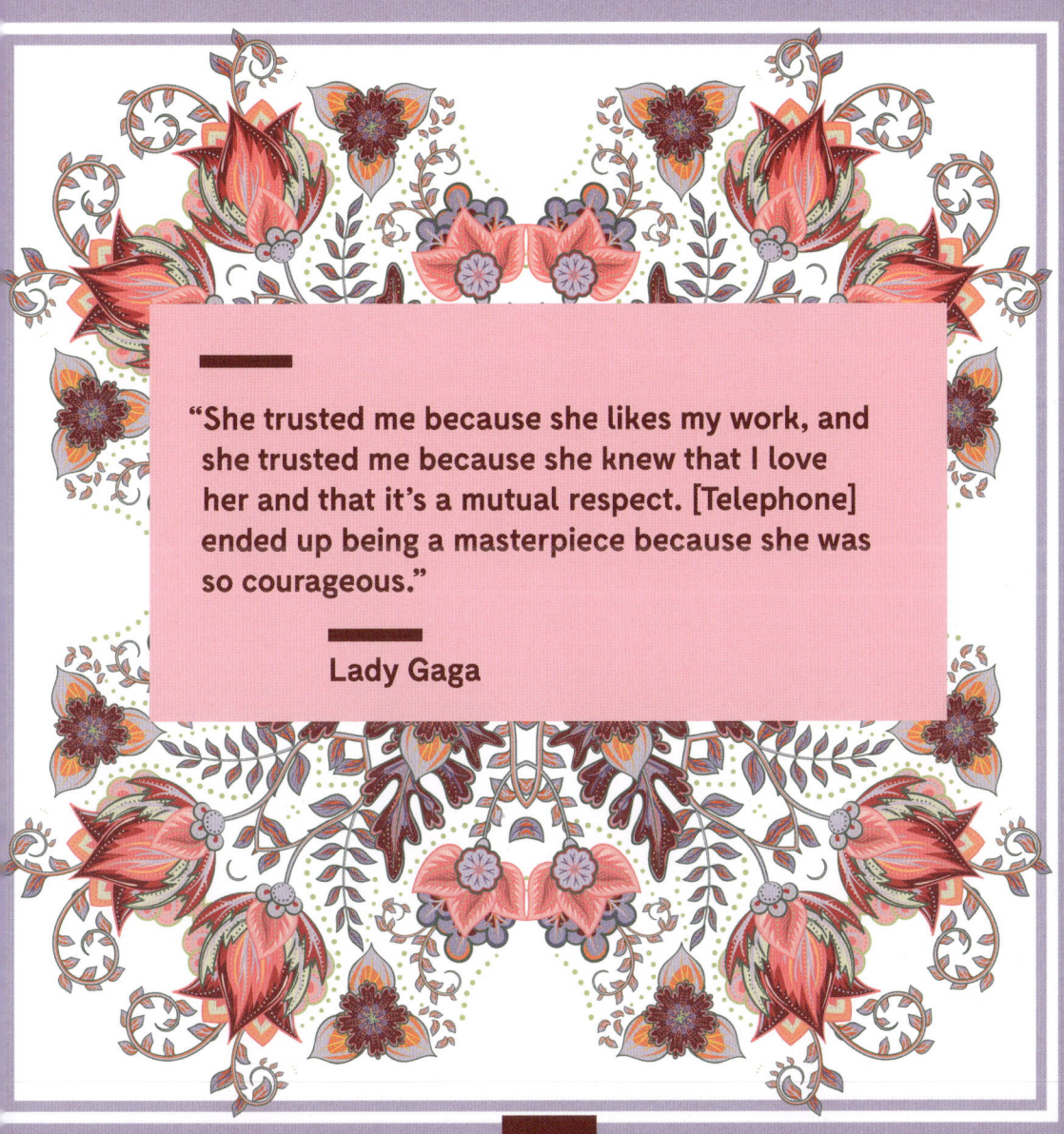

"She trusted me because she likes my work, and she trusted me because she knew that I love her and that it's a mutual respect. [Telephone] ended up being a masterpiece because she was so courageous."

Lady Gaga

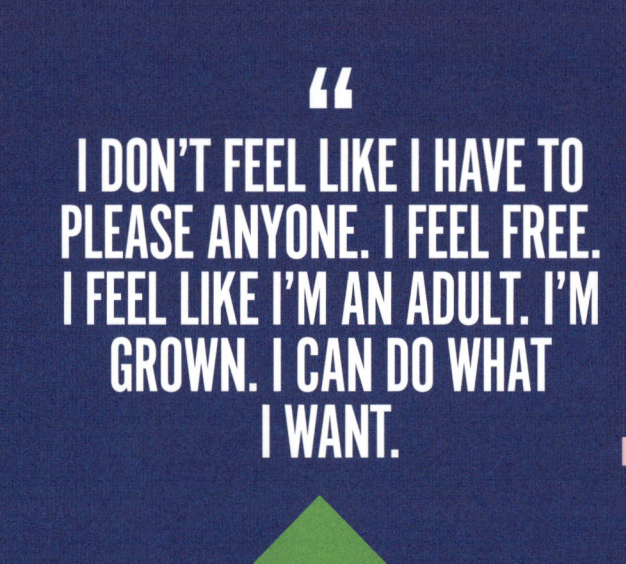

> "I DON'T FEEL LIKE I HAVE TO PLEASE ANYONE. I FEEL FREE. I FEEL LIKE I'M AN ADULT. I'M GROWN. I CAN DO WHAT I WANT.

> I CAN SAY WHAT I WANT. I CAN RETIRE IF I WANT. THAT'S WHY I'VE WORKED HARD. "

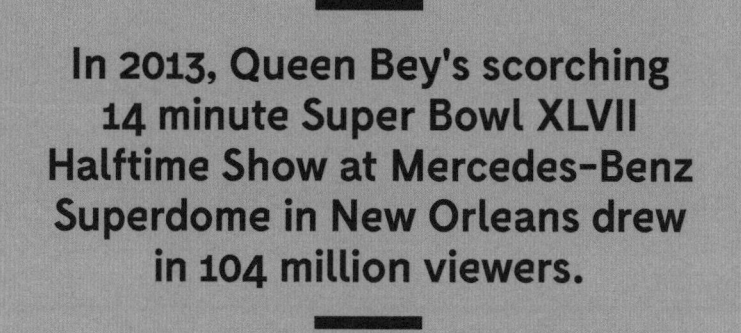

In 2013, Queen Bey's scorching 14 minute Super Bowl XLVII Halftime Show at Mercedes-Benz Superdome in New Orleans drew in 104 million viewers.

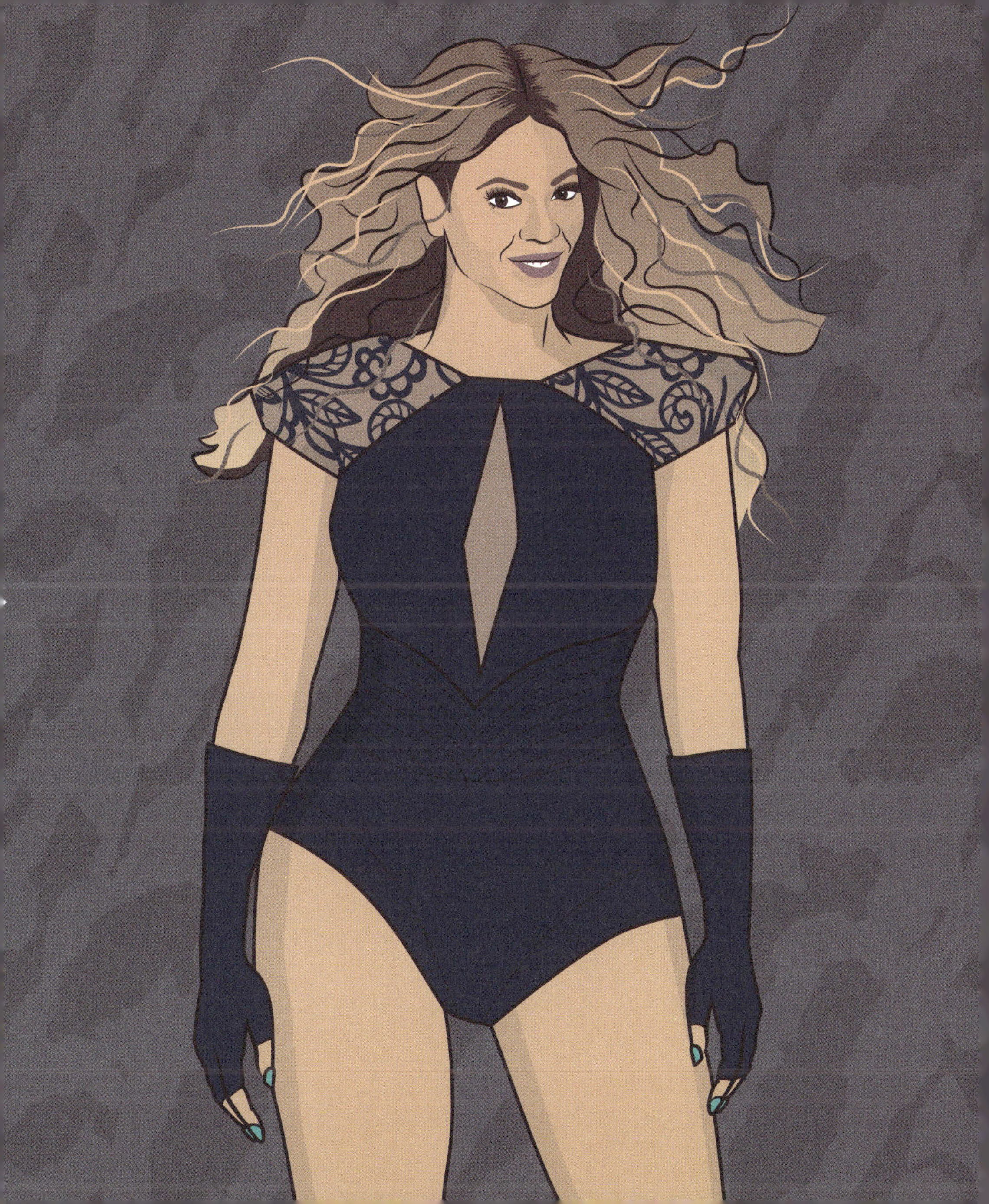

The 2013 Super Bowl performance featured a stage shaped like two Beyoncés in profile, with a giant fire Beyoncé towering above.

Bey was joined on stage by her former Destiny's Child bandmates Kelly Rowland and Michelle Williams to perform 'Bootylicious', 'Independent Women Part I' and 'Single Ladies'.

Hamish Hamilton, director of the Super Bowl XLVII halftime show, said of working with Beyoncé: "She can be a very benevolent dictator, she can also be a wonderful collaborator. Through the process you meet both sides. She has such ambition to be perfect, to be the best, that you just get swept up along in that."

In a feat of masterful promotion, Beyoncé managed to record her entire groundbreaking visual album, *Lemonade*, in secret and launch it as a surprise special on HBO. The album has since been exclusively available to stream through Tidal – a company co-created by Jay Z (and part-owned by Bey) as an artist-owned streaming service with the mission of paying higher royalties to musical artists and songwriters.

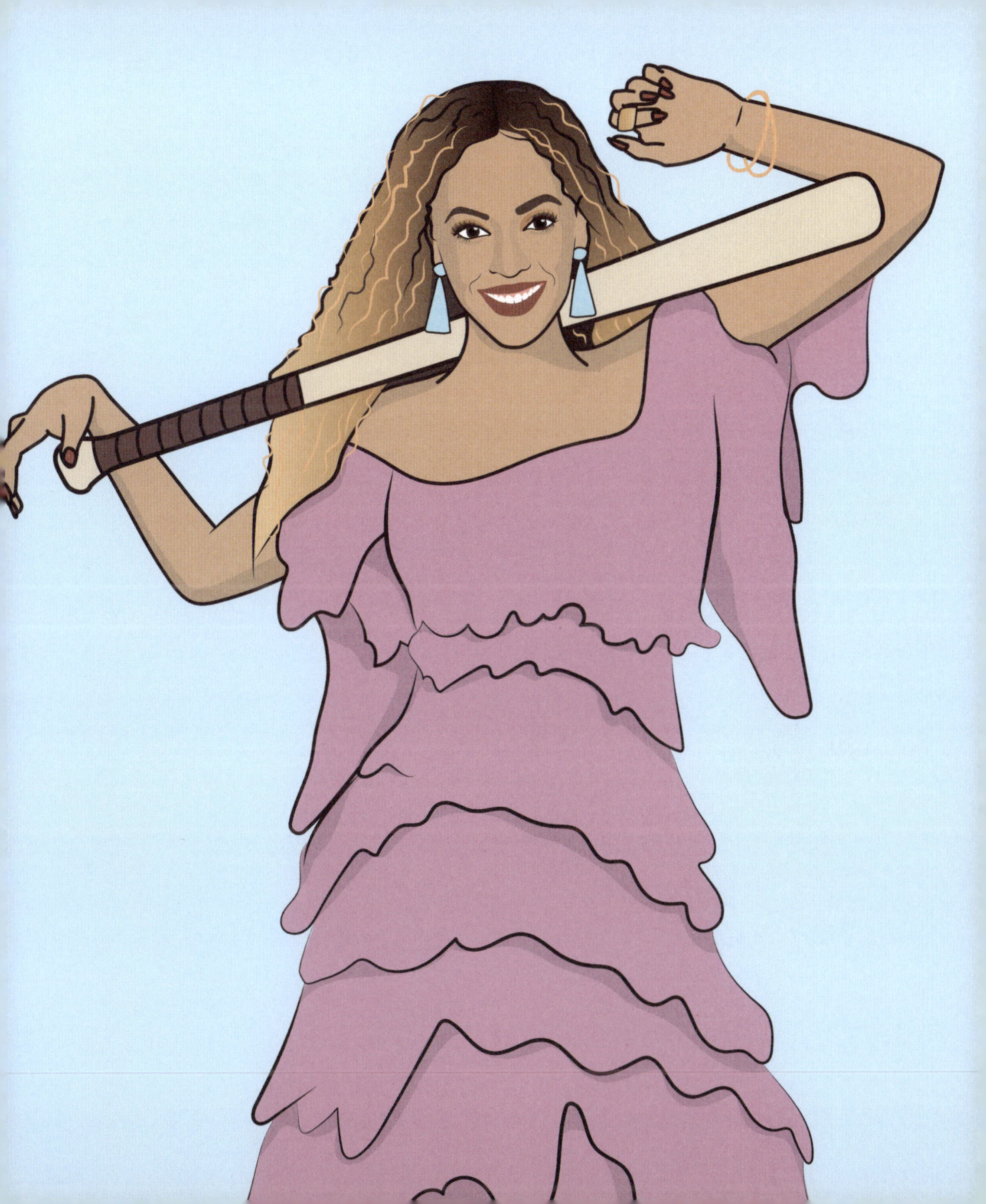

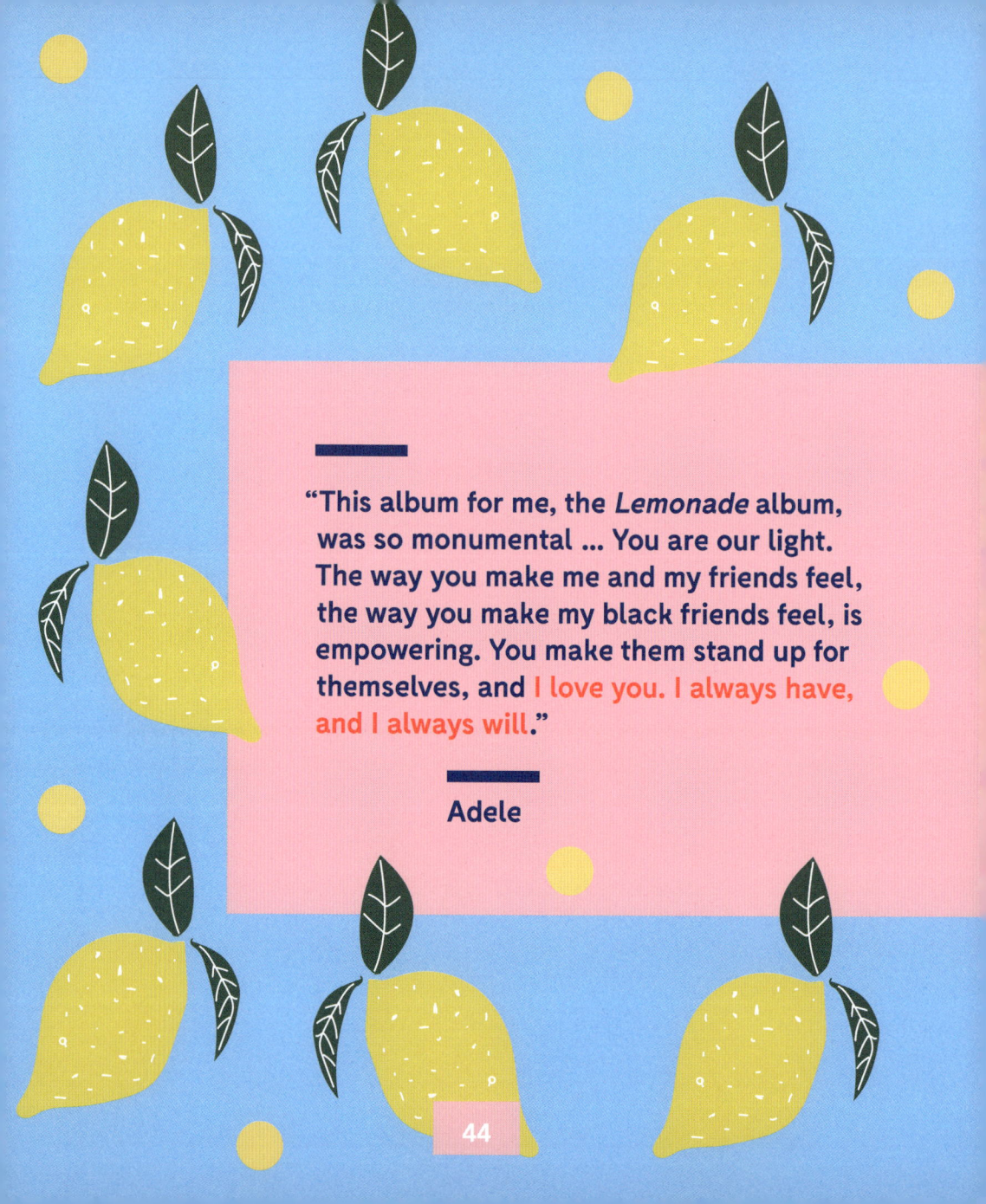

"This album for me, the *Lemonade* album, was so monumental ... You are our light. The way you make me and my friends feel, the way you make my black friends feel, is empowering. You make them stand up for themselves, and I love you. I always have, and I always will."

Adele

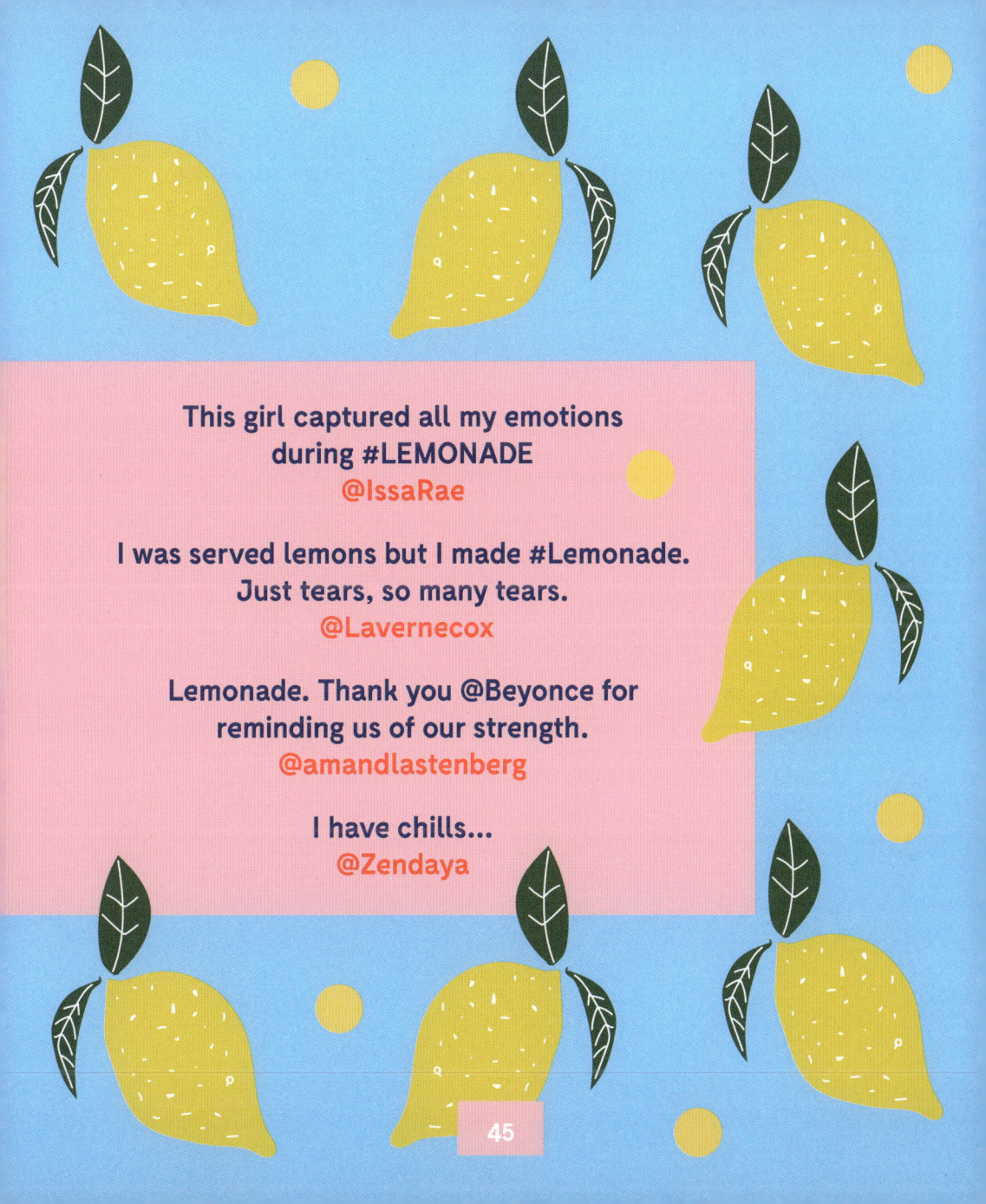

This girl captured all my emotions
during #LEMONADE
@IssaRae

I was served lemons but I made #Lemonade.
Just tears, so many tears.
@Lavernecox

Lemonade. Thank you @Beyonce for
reminding us of our strength.
@amandlastenberg

I have chills…
@Zendaya

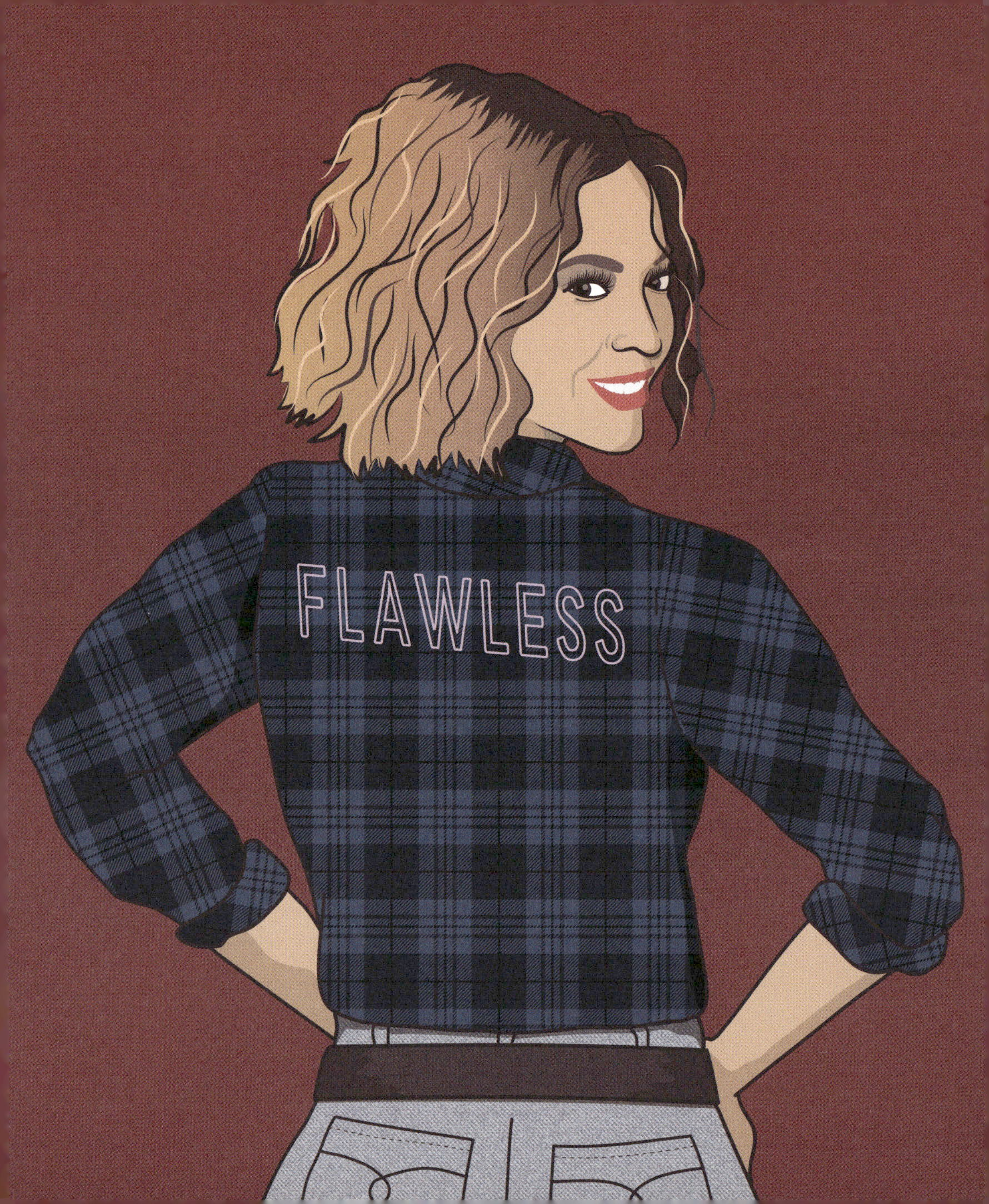
FLAWLESS

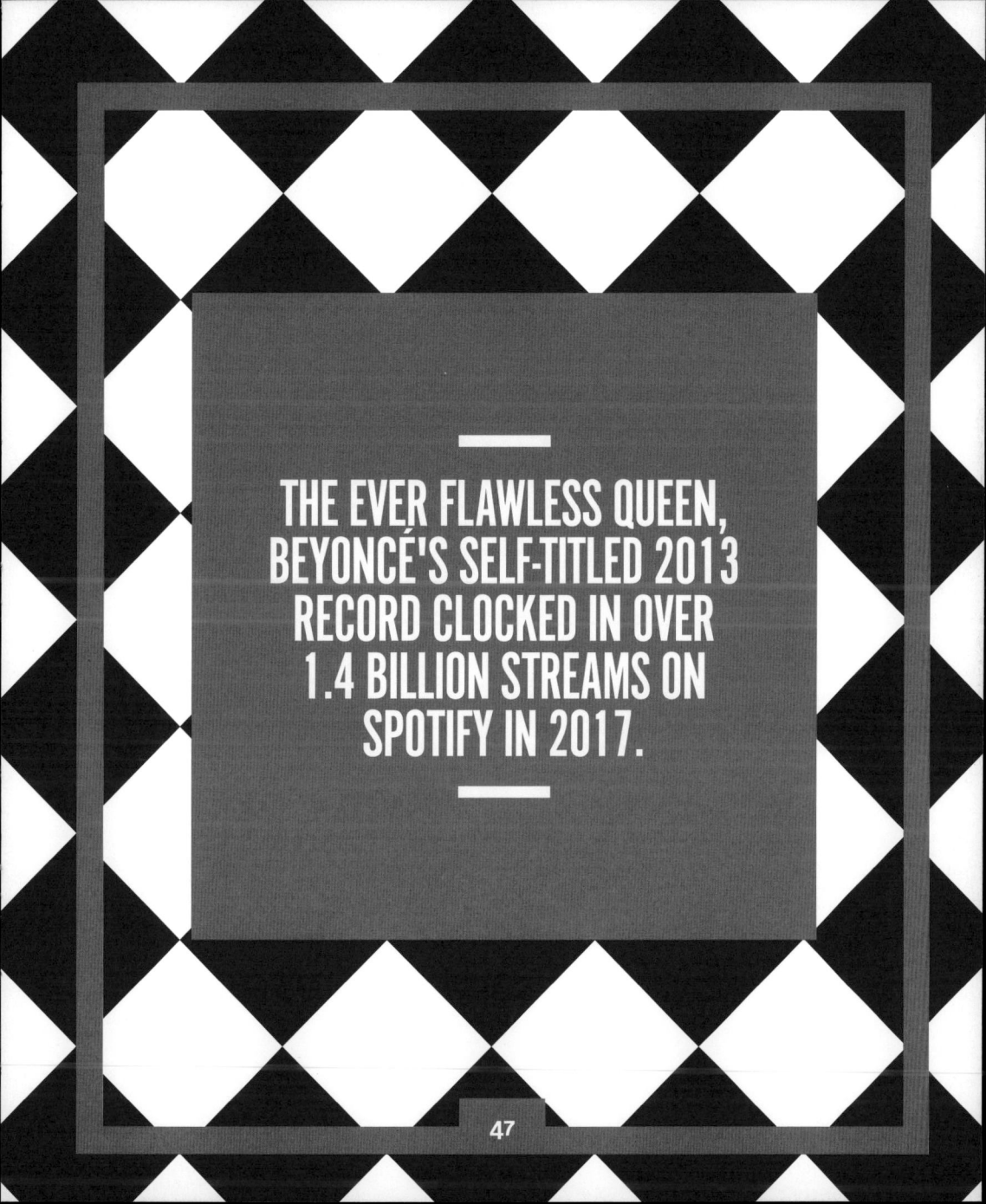

THE EVER FLAWLESS QUEEN, BEYONCÉ'S SELF-TITLED 2013 RECORD CLOCKED IN OVER 1.4 BILLION STREAMS ON SPOTIFY IN 2017.

"She is an animal on stage, where she embodies this utterly instinctive beauty. [On] tour, there were more than 500 people in her entourage who didn't stop talking during rehearsals, but when there was even the slightest decision to make, she was able to shut out all the noise and focus like a tiger on a lamb."

Thierry Mugler

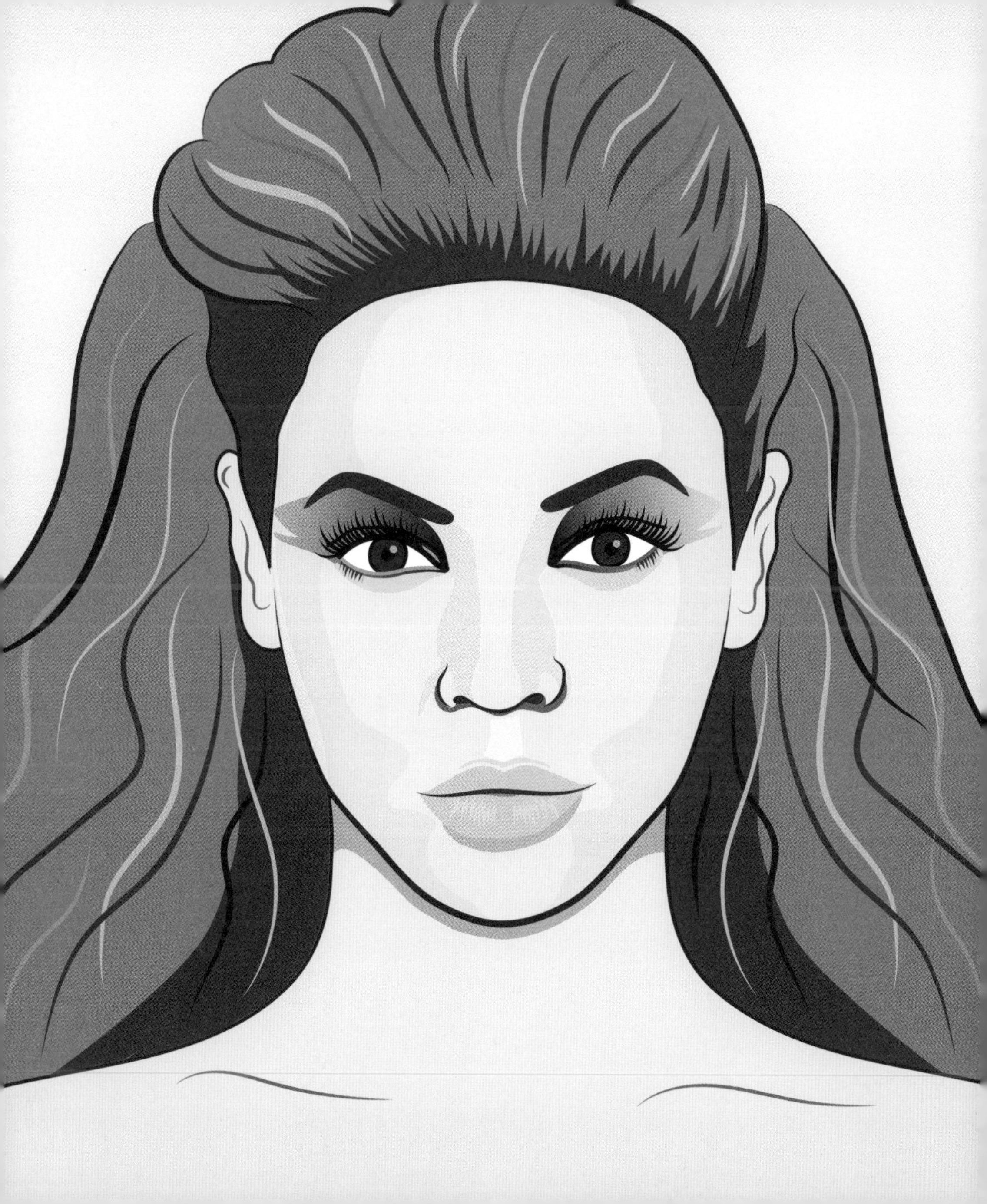

Beyoncé returned to the Super Bowl stage in 2016 for the Super Bowl 50 Halftime Show, at Levi's Stadium in Santa Clara, California. She was slated as a guest star, supporting Coldplay's headline act, but, along with fellow guest Bruno Mars, she managed to completely and entirely steal the show.

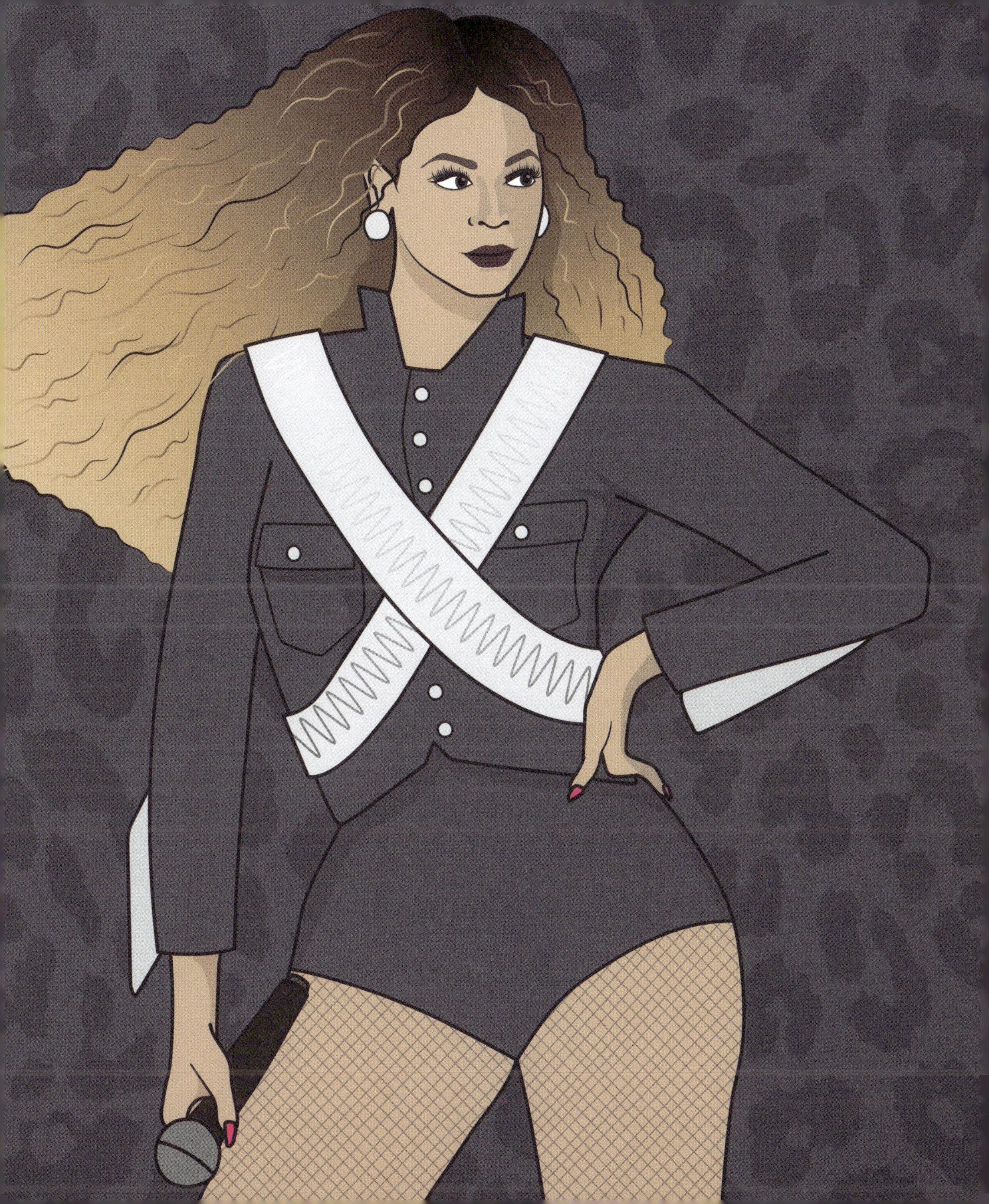

Beyoncé dropped the boldly political video for 'Formation' one day before the 2016 Super Bowl and then slayed in a performance of the song that was rich in symbolism referencing black culture and celebrating black feminity.

Her back-up dancers rocked afros, and wore costumes and raised their fists in a way that clearly referenced the Black Panthers. The choreography featured an X formation that many believed was a tribute to civil rights leader Malcolm X, and Bey's costume was a clear nod to Michael Jackson's legendary 1993 Super Bowl performance.

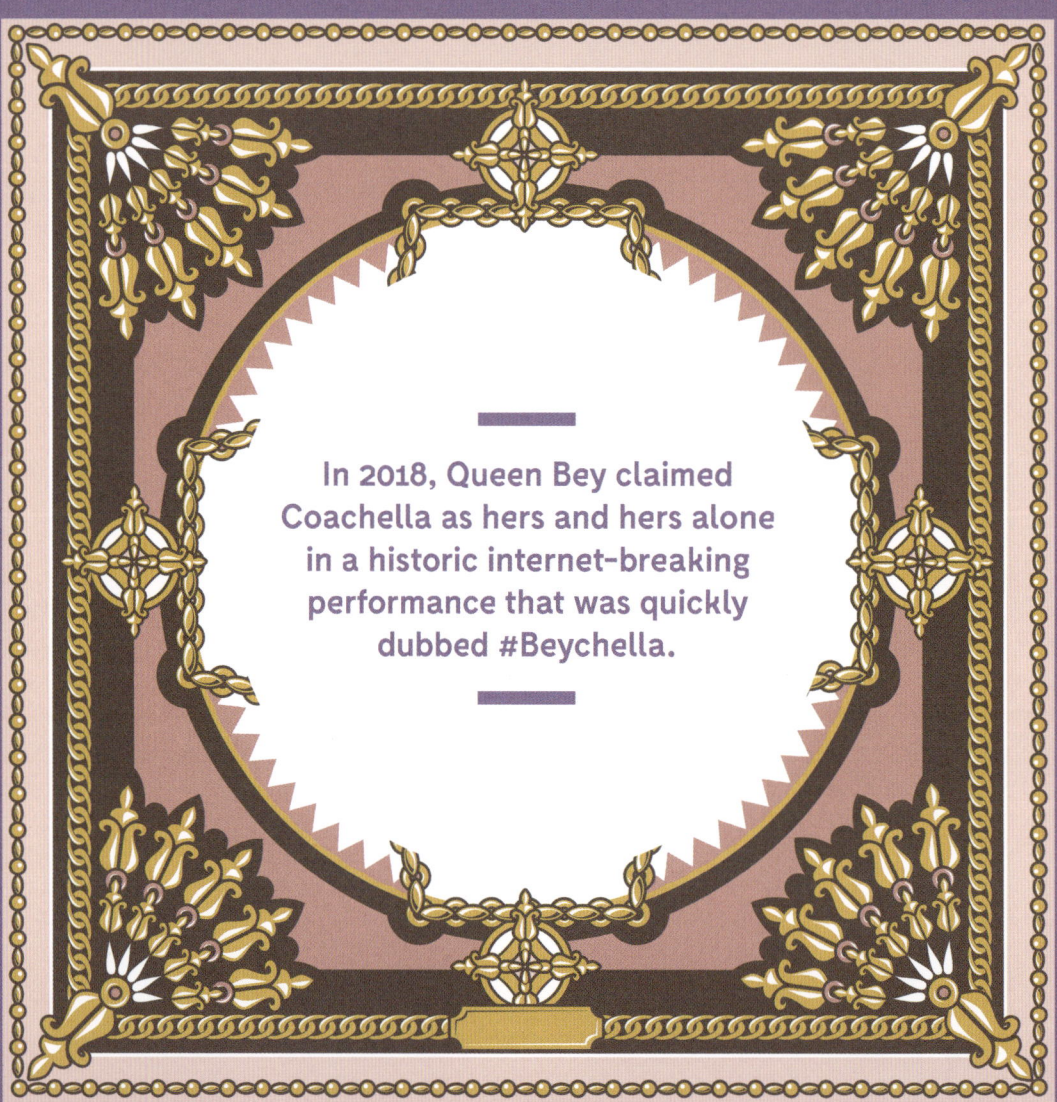

COACHELLA IS OBLITERATED.

In 2018, Queen Bey claimed Coachella as hers and hers alone in a historic internet-breaking performance that was quickly dubbed #Beychella.

COACHELLA IS OBLITERATED.

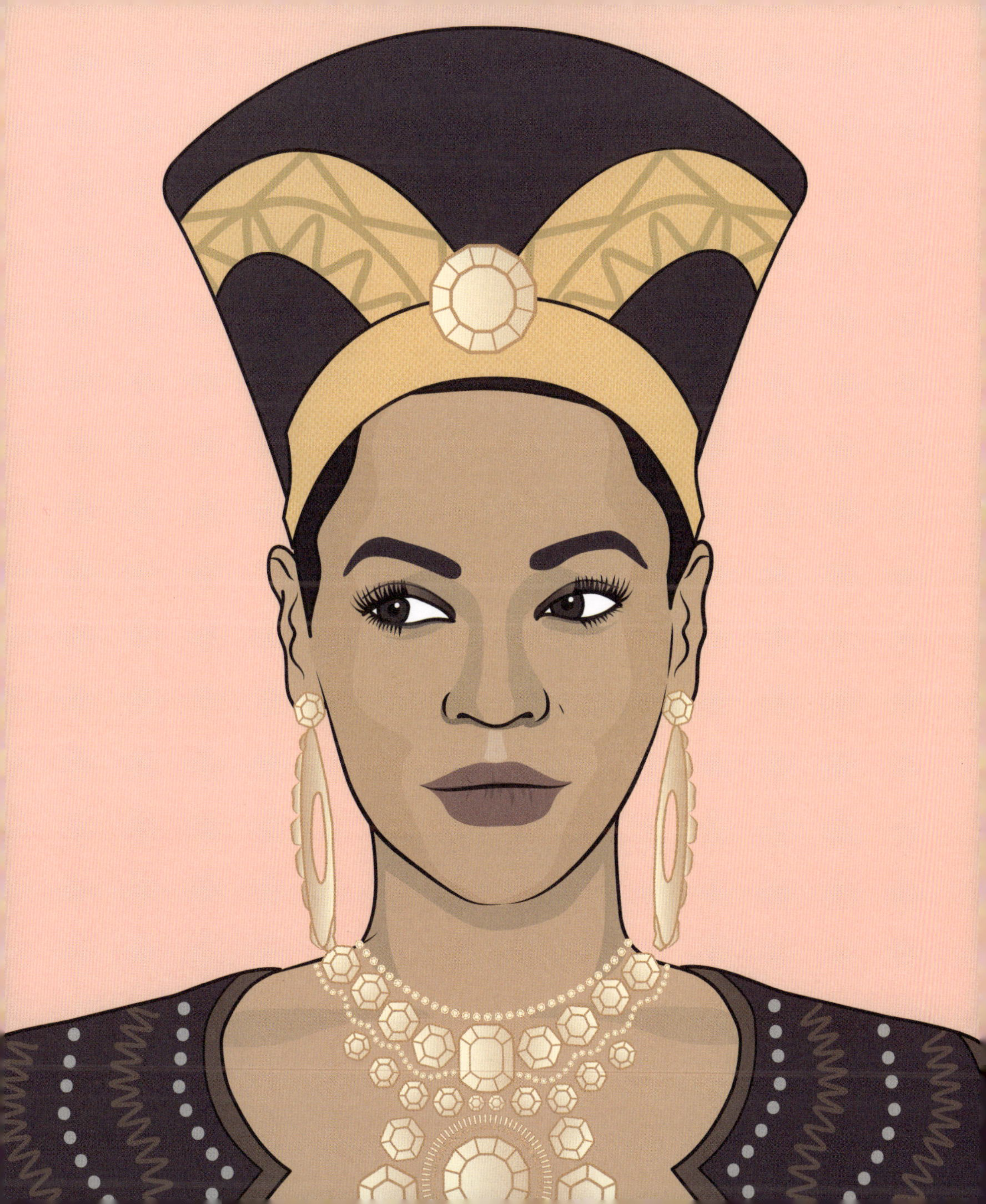

Not only was Beyoncé the first African-American woman to headline Coachella, she did so with a two hour, 27-song set, complete with 100 back-up dancers, a 200-person marching band, five custom-designed Balmain costume changes and special guests Destiny's Child, Jay Z and Solange Knowles. The show heavily referenced historically black colleges and universities (HBCUs), and Bey paid tribute to Nina Simone by covering 'Lilac Wine' as well as singing the black national anthem, 'Lift Every Voice and Sing'.

Then, a week later, she did it all again.

Because Queen Bey is here to slay, rather than exactly replicating her show on the second weekend of the festival — as any mere mortal would do — Beyoncé returned with all new takes on her heavily symbolic jaw-dropping Balmain looks.

QUEE[N]

BOW[...]

> "I'M LEARNING HOW TO DROWN OUT THE CONSTANT NOISE THAT IS SUCH AN INSEPARABLE PART OF MY LIFE. I DON'T HAVE TO PROVE ANYTHING TO ANYONE, I ONLY HAVE TO FOLLOW MY HEART AND CONCENTRATE ON WHAT I WANT TO SAY TO THE WORLD. **I RUN MY WORLD.**"

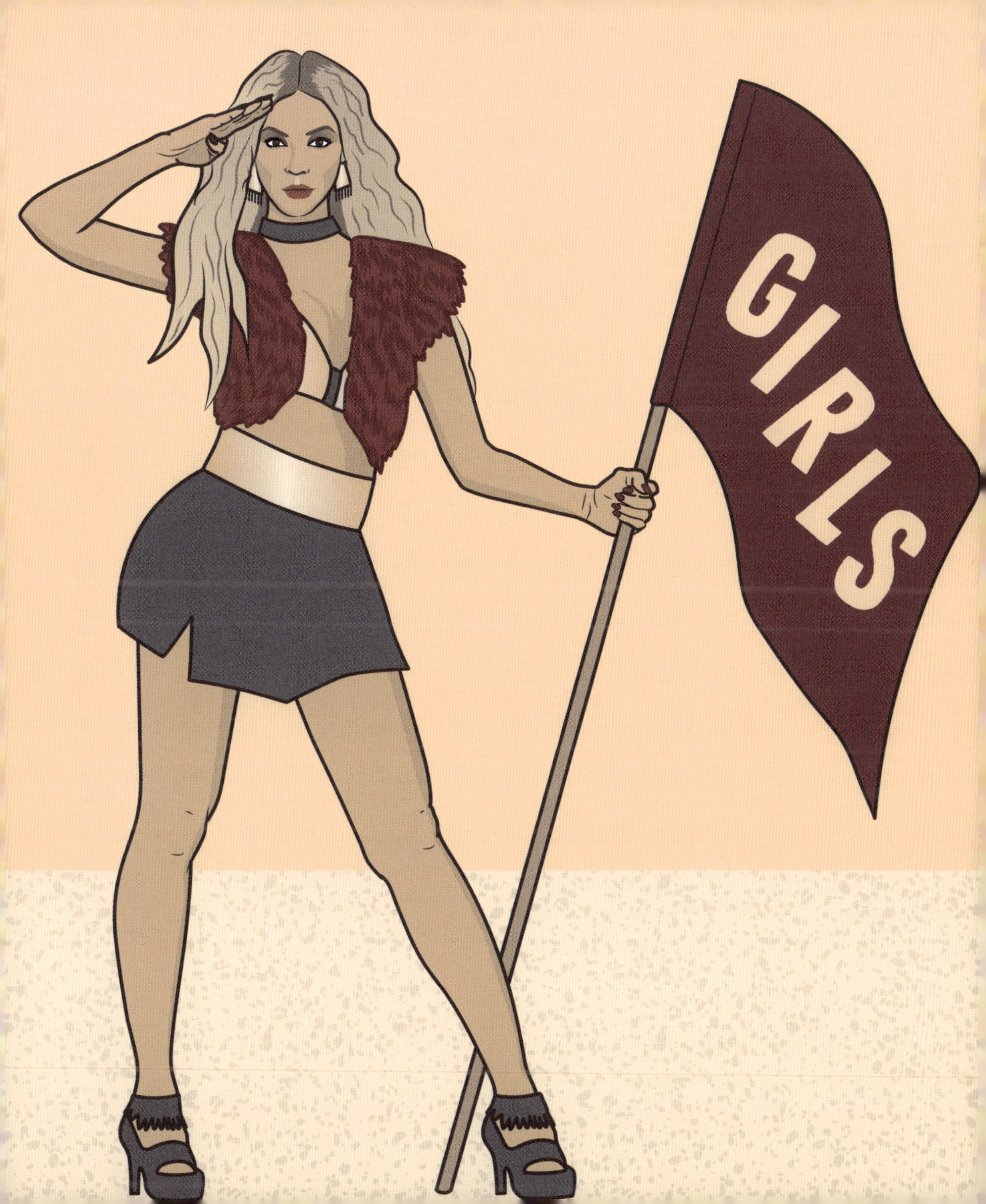
GIRLS

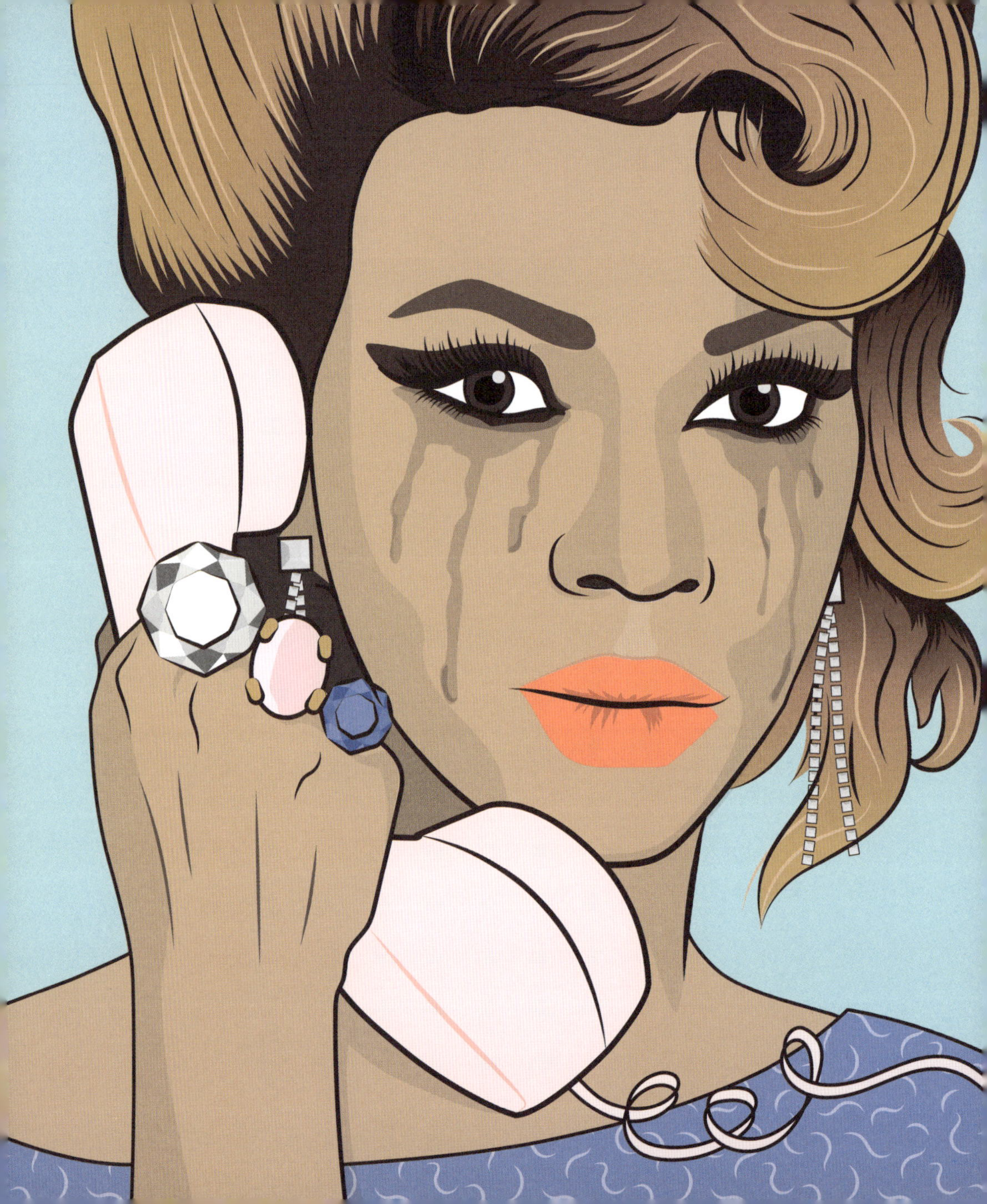

> I'm not afraid to make a mistake. I embrace mistakes. They make you who you are. I've never been afraid to fall.

Singing 'At Last' for President Barack Obama on his inauguration night in 2009 is one of Beyoncé's proudest moments, as a singer and as an American.

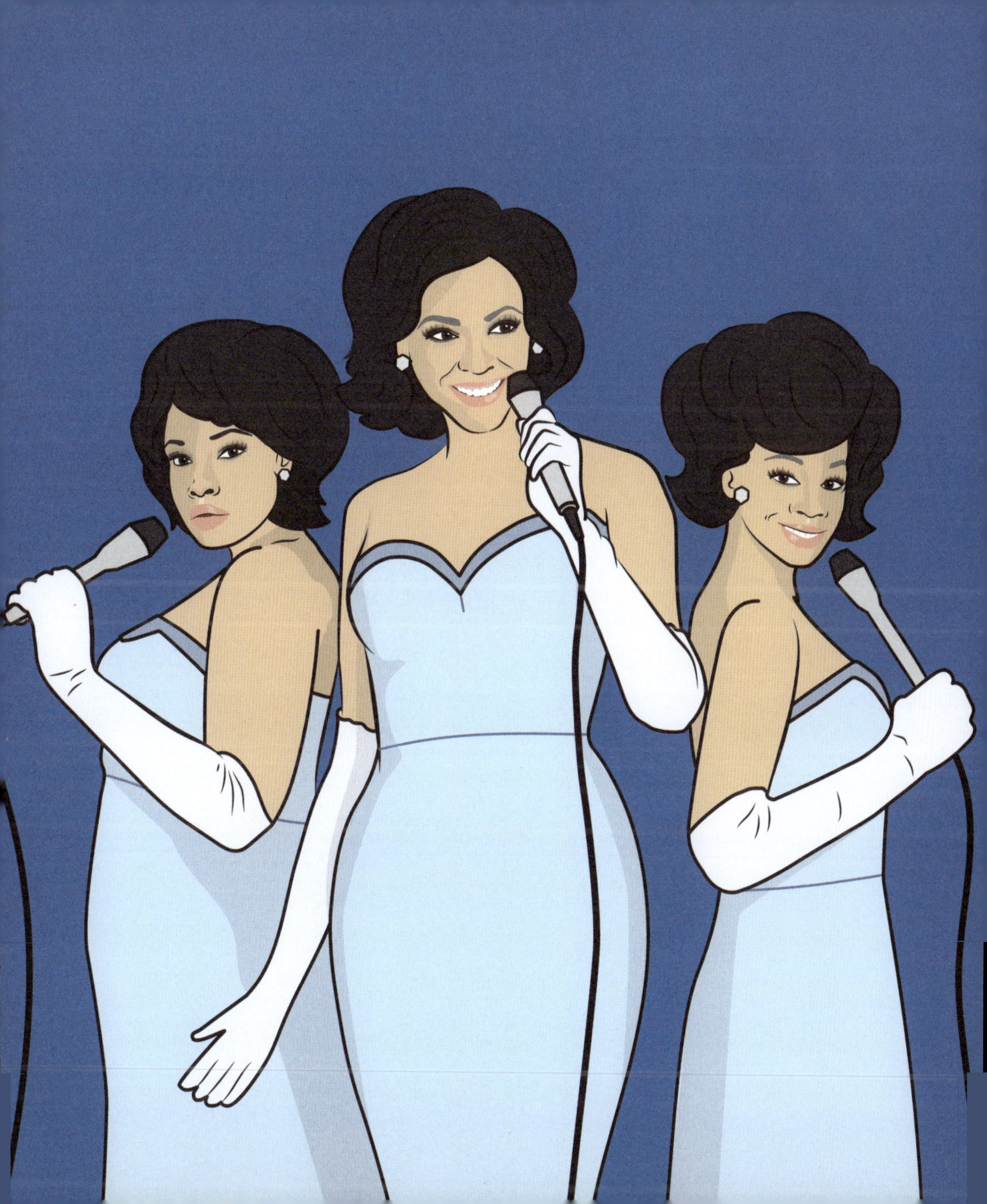

ON HER ALTER EGO, SASCHA FIERCE ...

2008

"I have someone else that takes over when it's time for me to work, and when I'm on stage, this alter ego I created that kind of protects me and who I really am. Sasha Fierce is the fun, more sensual, more aggressive, more outspoken and more glamorous side that comes out when I'm working and when I'm on the stage."

2013

"I killed off needing Sasha Fierce. I don't need her anymore. I am Sasha Fierce. It's interesting because now I've done it for so long it's so easy for me to go into that performance mode ... I don't have to mentally prepare myself for it. Honestly, I'm much more interested in showing people the sensitive, the passionate, and the compassionate person that I am. More so than Sasha Fierce."

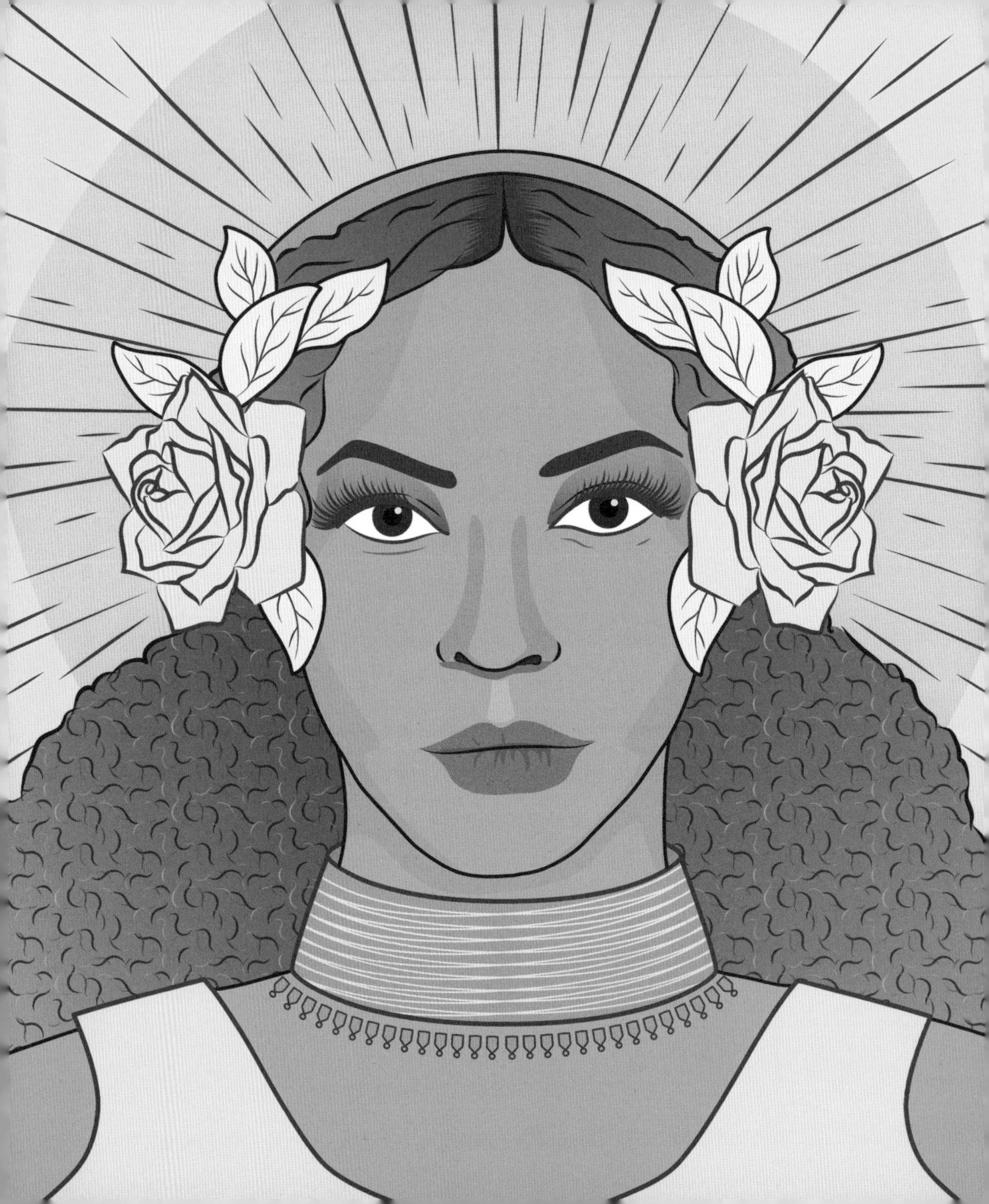

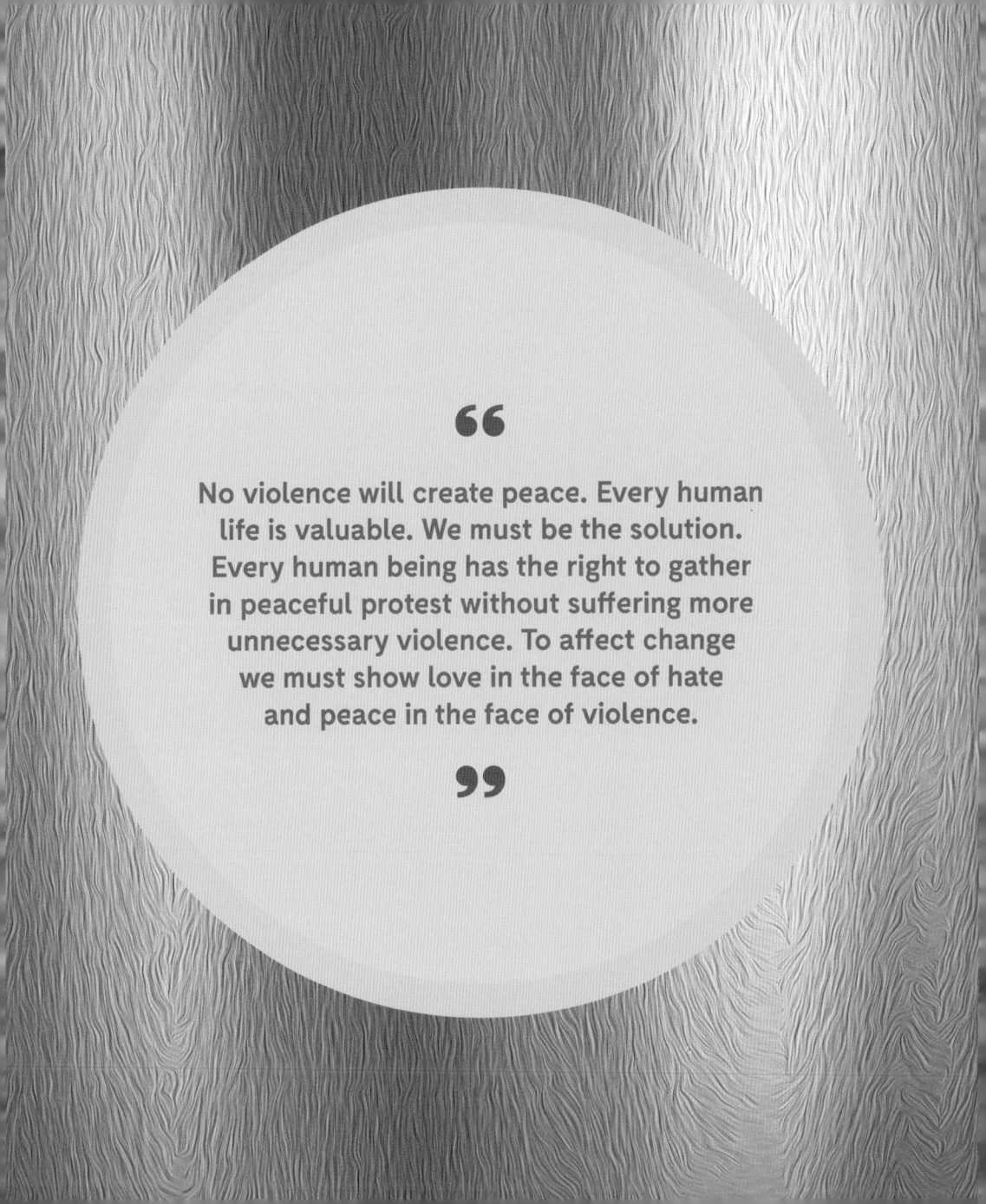

> No violence will create peace. Every human life is valuable. We must be the solution. Every human being has the right to gather in peaceful protest without suffering more unnecessary violence. To affect change we must show love in the face of hate and peace in the face of violence.

> "WOMEN ARE MORE THAN 50 PER CENT OF THE POPULATION AND MORE THAN 50 PER CENT OF VOTERS. WE MUST DEMAND THAT WE ALL RECEIVE 100 PER CENT OF THE OPPORTUNITIES."

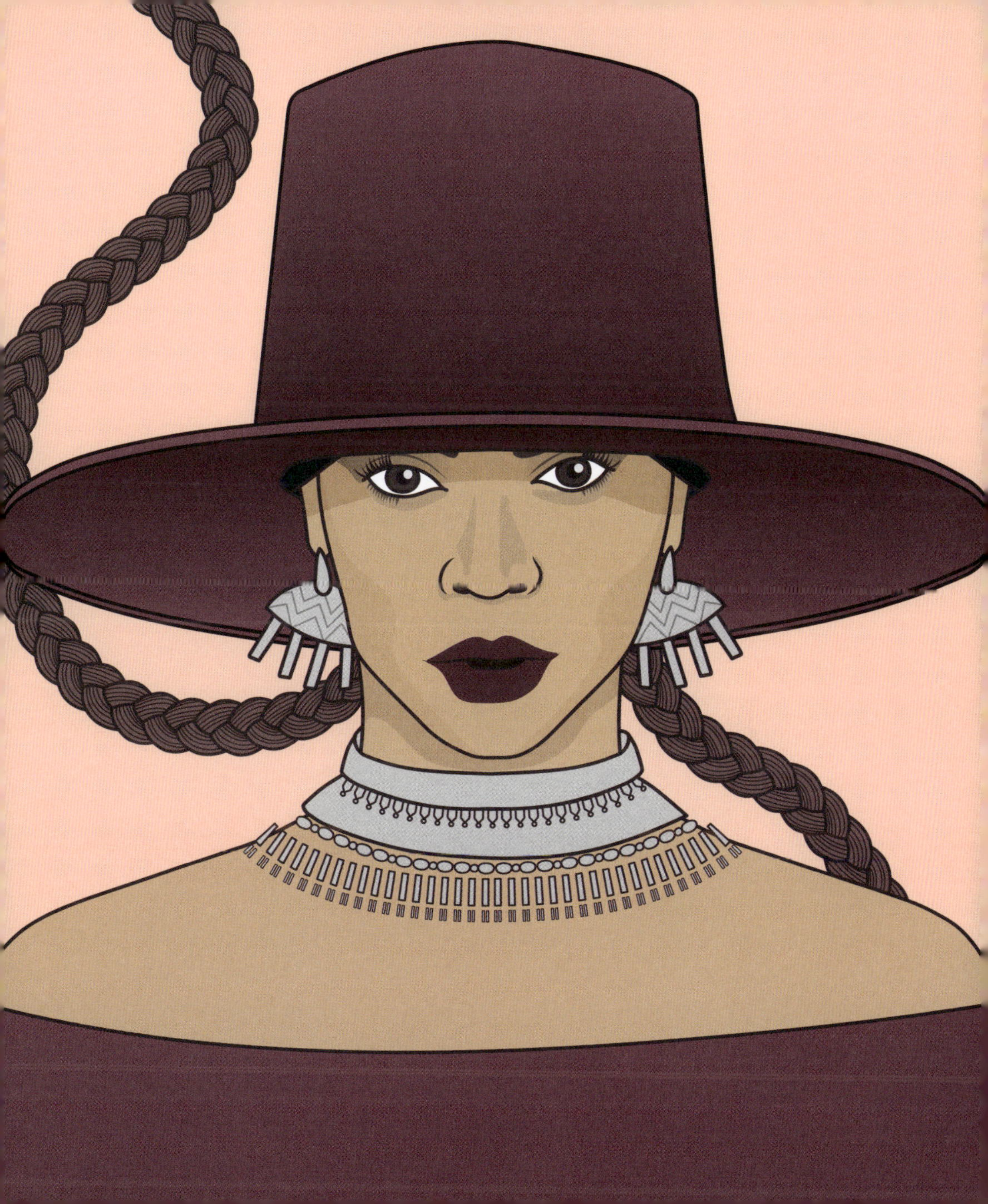

> "I don't like to gamble, but if there's one thing I'm willing to bet on, **it's myself.**"

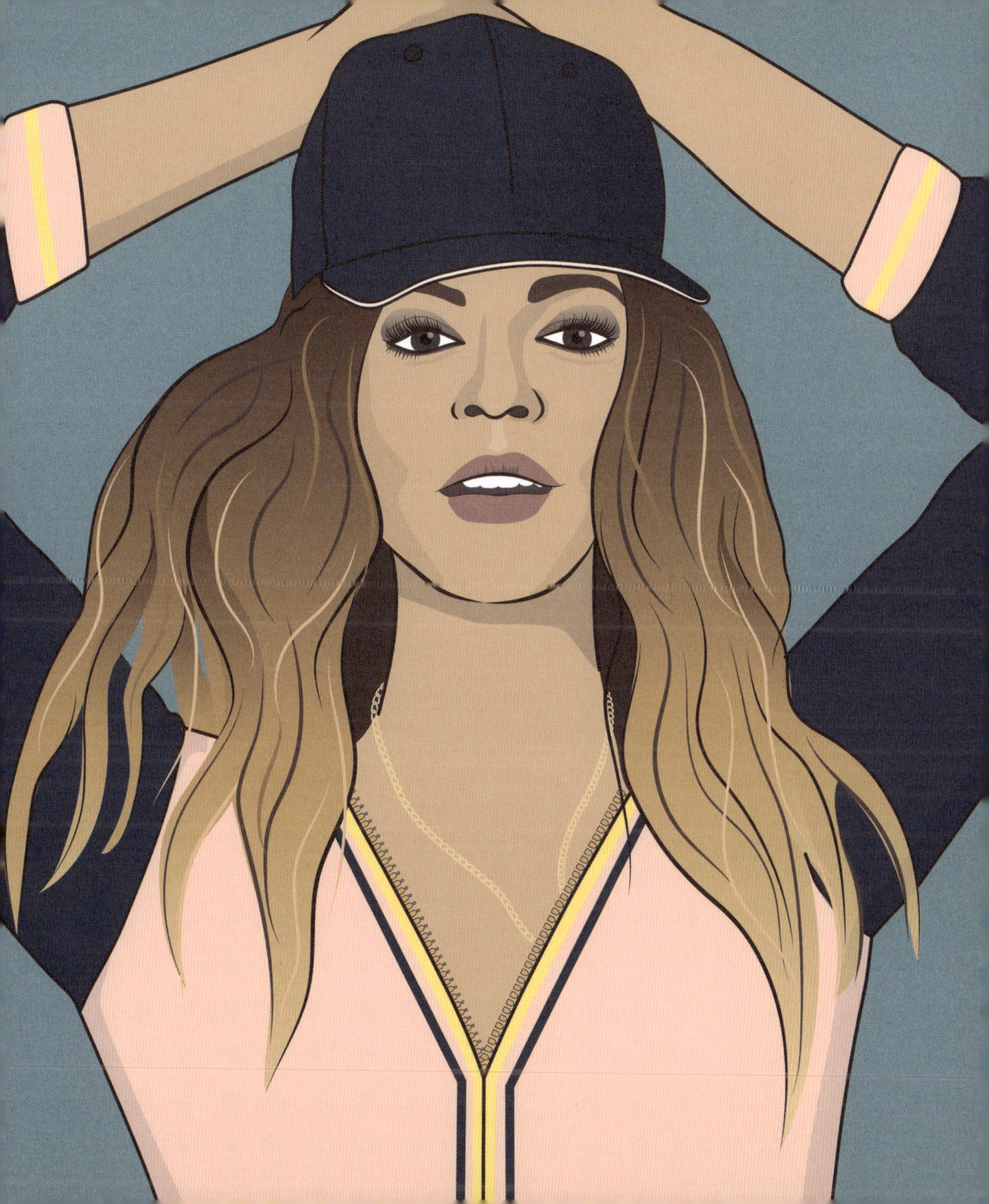

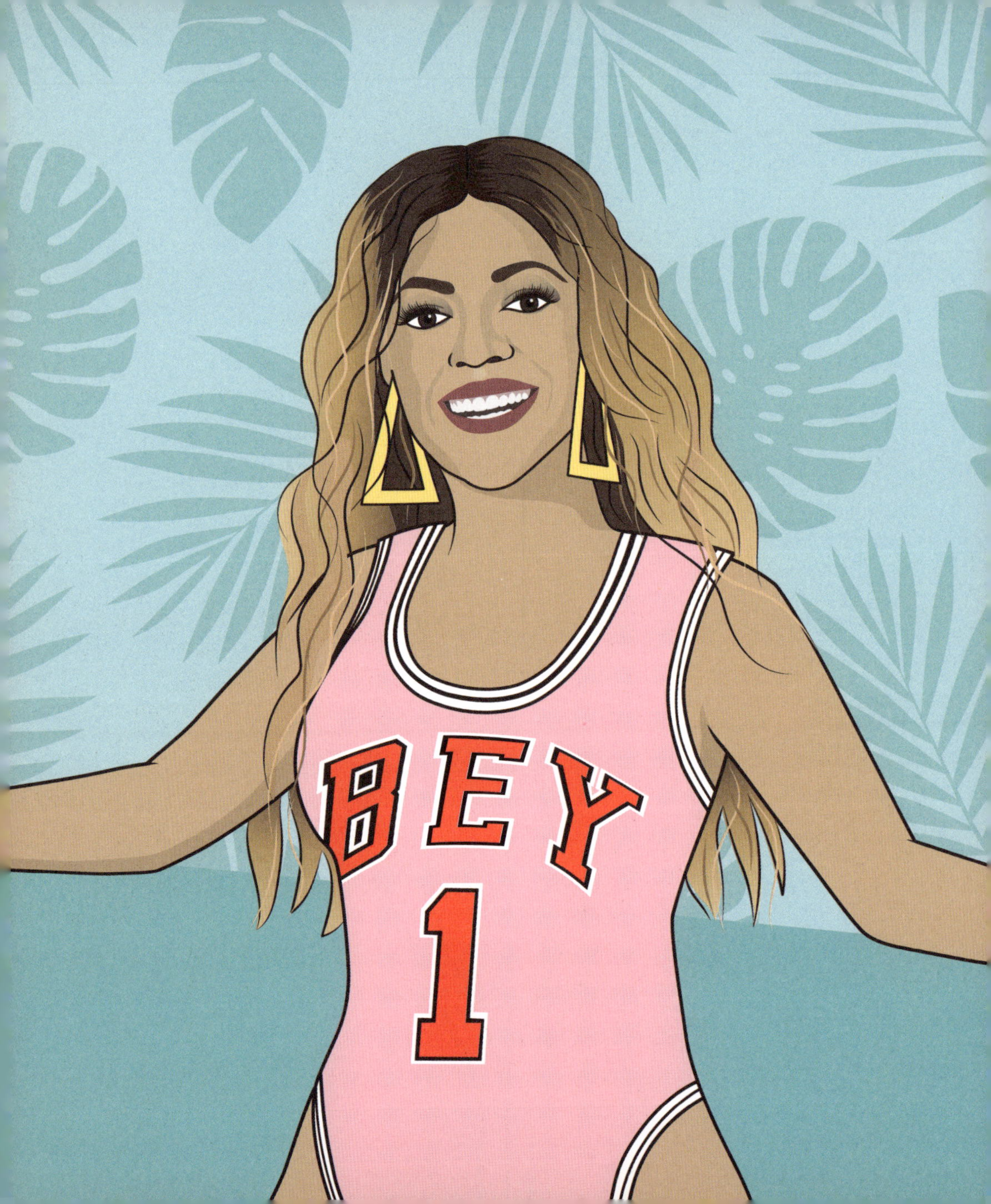
BEY
1

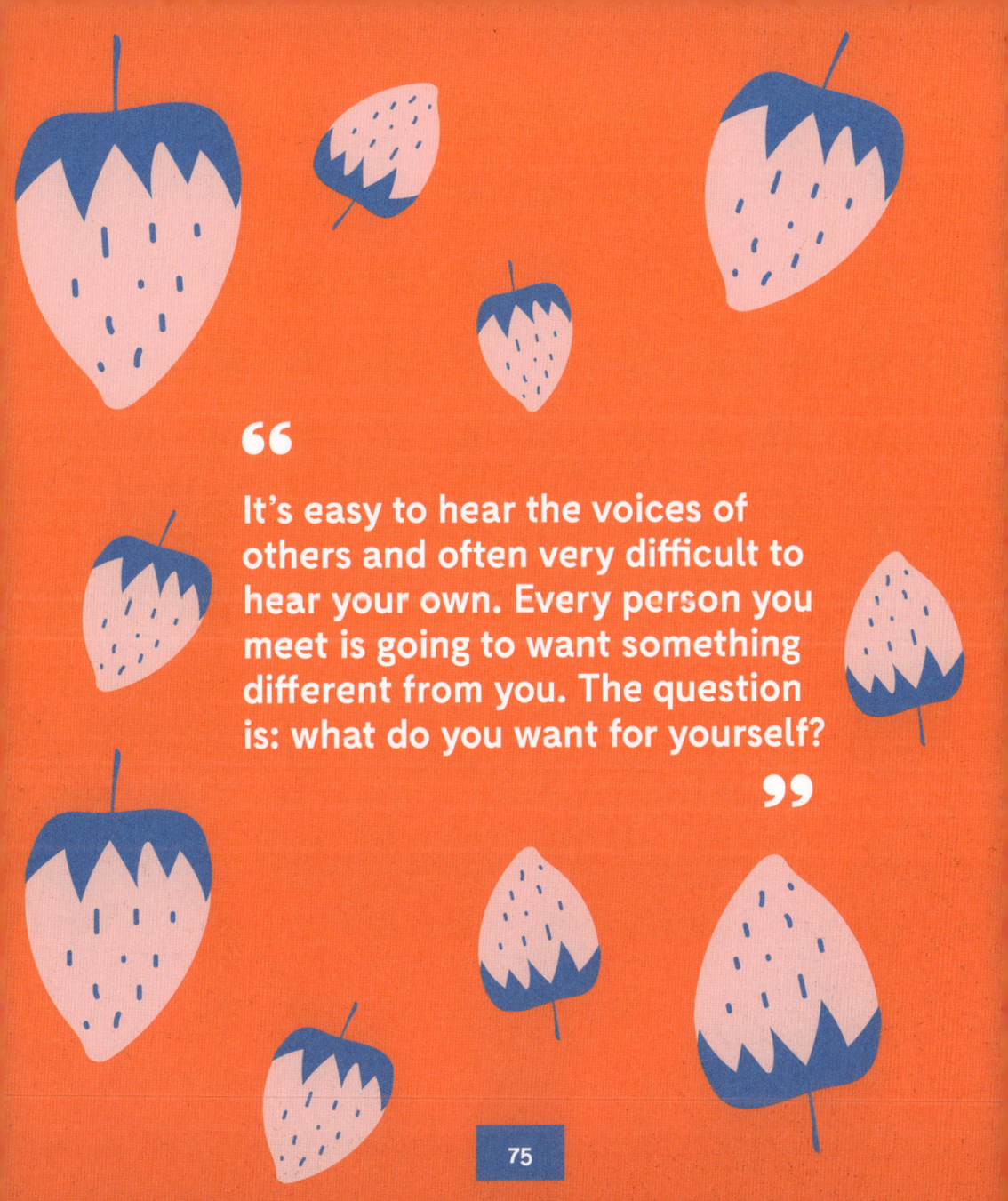

> It's easy to hear the voices of others and often very difficult to hear your own. Every person you meet is going to want something different from you. The question is: what do you want for yourself?

> "
> WE'RE NOT ALL JUST ONE THING. EVERYONE WHO BELIEVES IN EQUAL RIGHTS FOR MEN AND WOMEN DOESN'T SPEAK THE SAME, OR DRESS THE SAME, OR THINK THE SAME. IF A MAN CAN DO IT, A WOMAN SHOULD BE ABLE TO. IT'S THAT SIMPLE.
> "

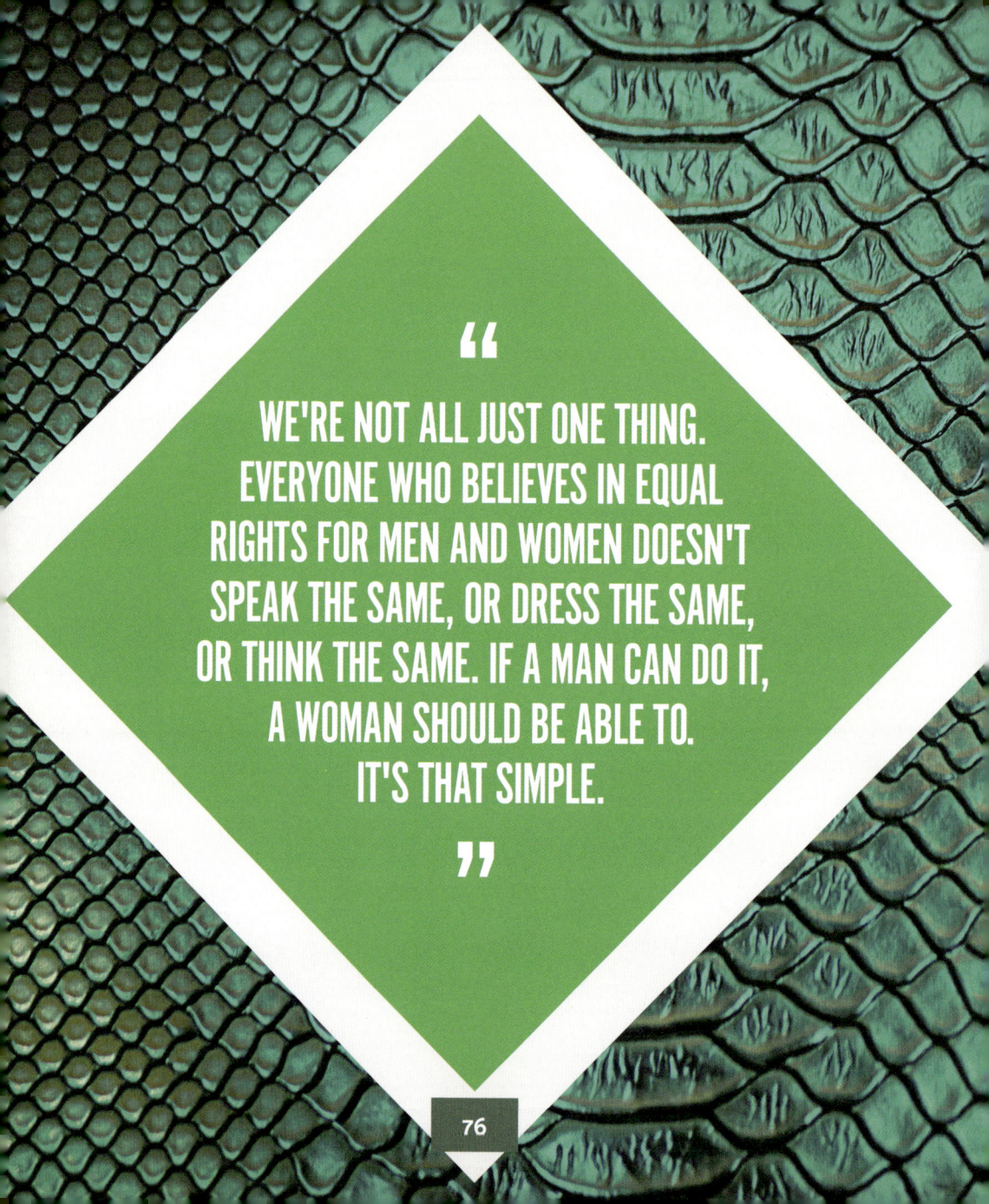

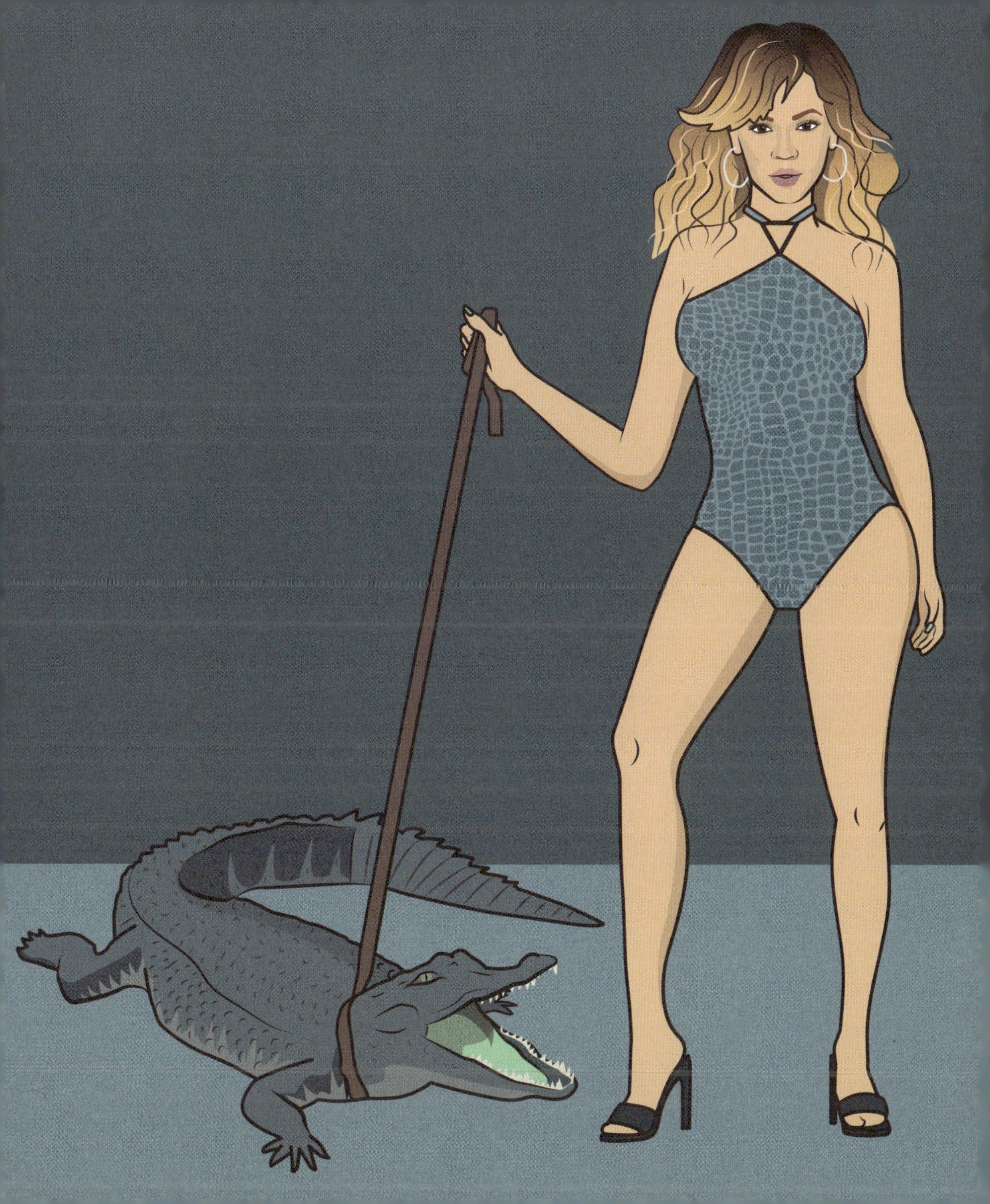

> **We have to teach our boys the rules of equality and respect, so that as they grow up gender equality becomes a natural way of life. And we have to teach our girls that they can reach as high as humanly possible.**

> It's important to me to show images to my children that reflect their beauty, so they can grow up in a world where they look in the mirror, first through their own families, as well as the news, the Super Bowl, the Olympics, the White House and the Grammys, and see themselves. And have no doubt that they're beautiful, intelligent and capable. This is something I want for every child of every race.

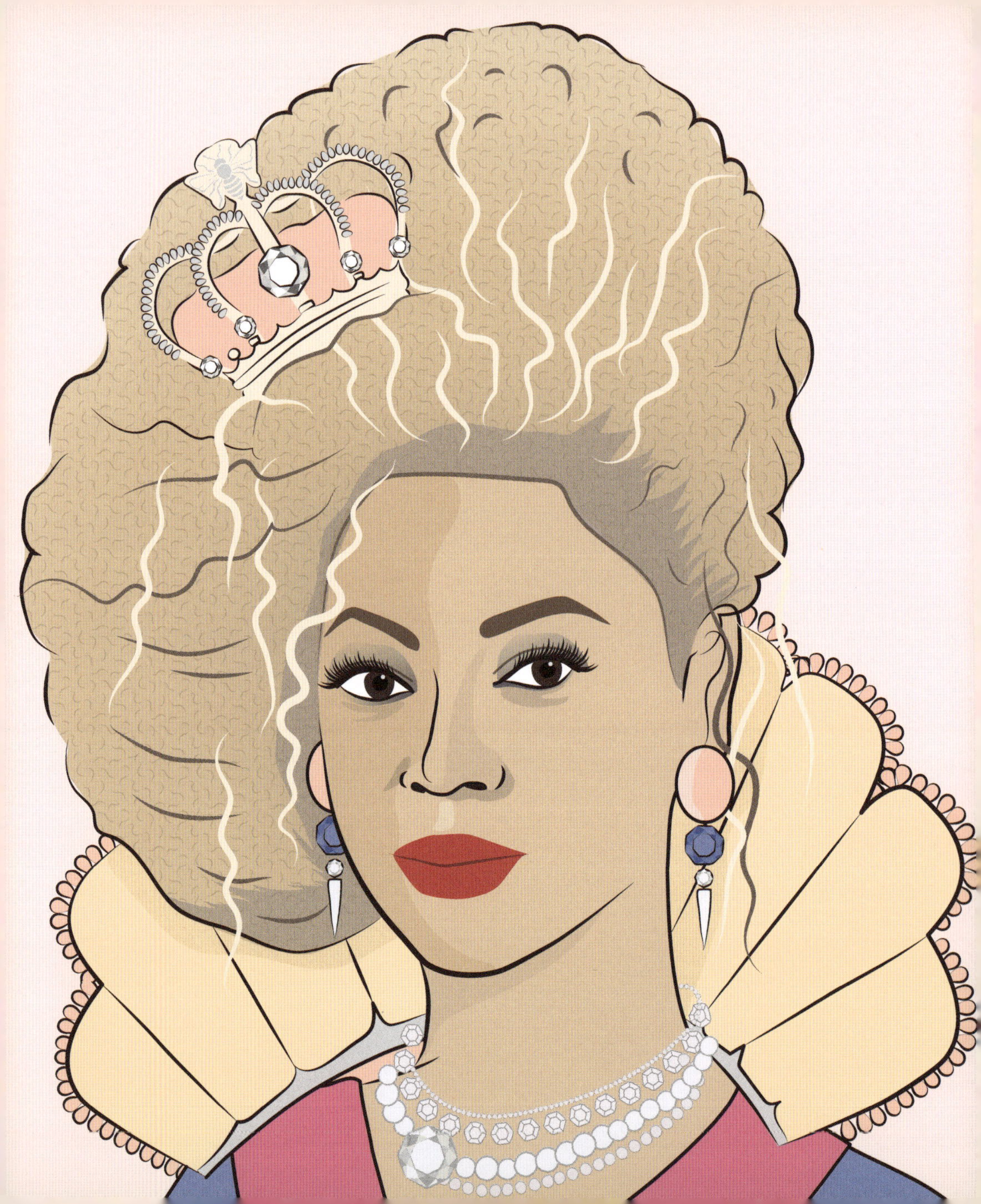

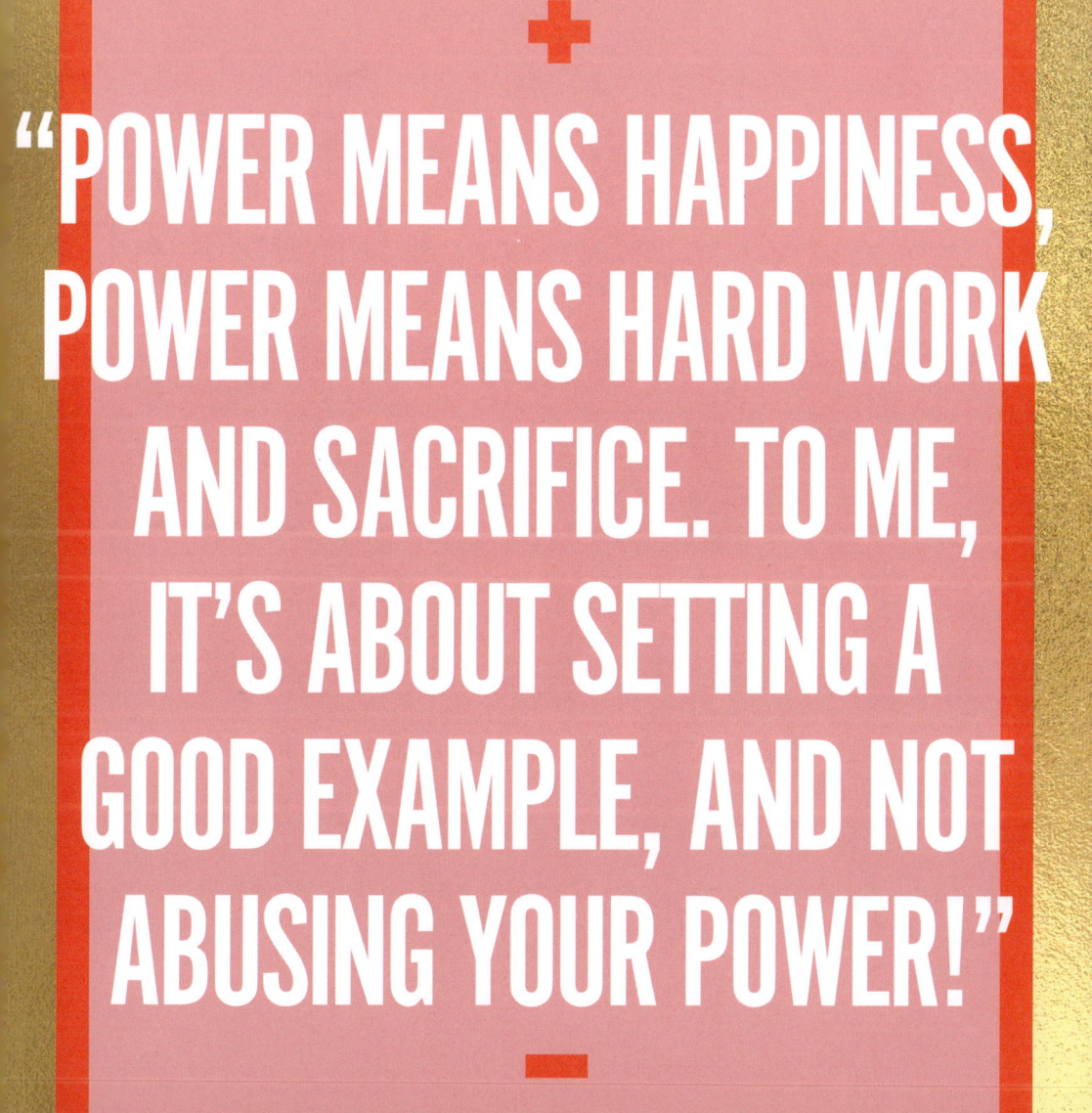

"POWER MEANS HAPPINESS, POWER MEANS HARD WORK AND SACRIFICE. TO ME, IT'S ABOUT SETTING A GOOD EXAMPLE, AND NOT ABUSING YOUR POWER!"

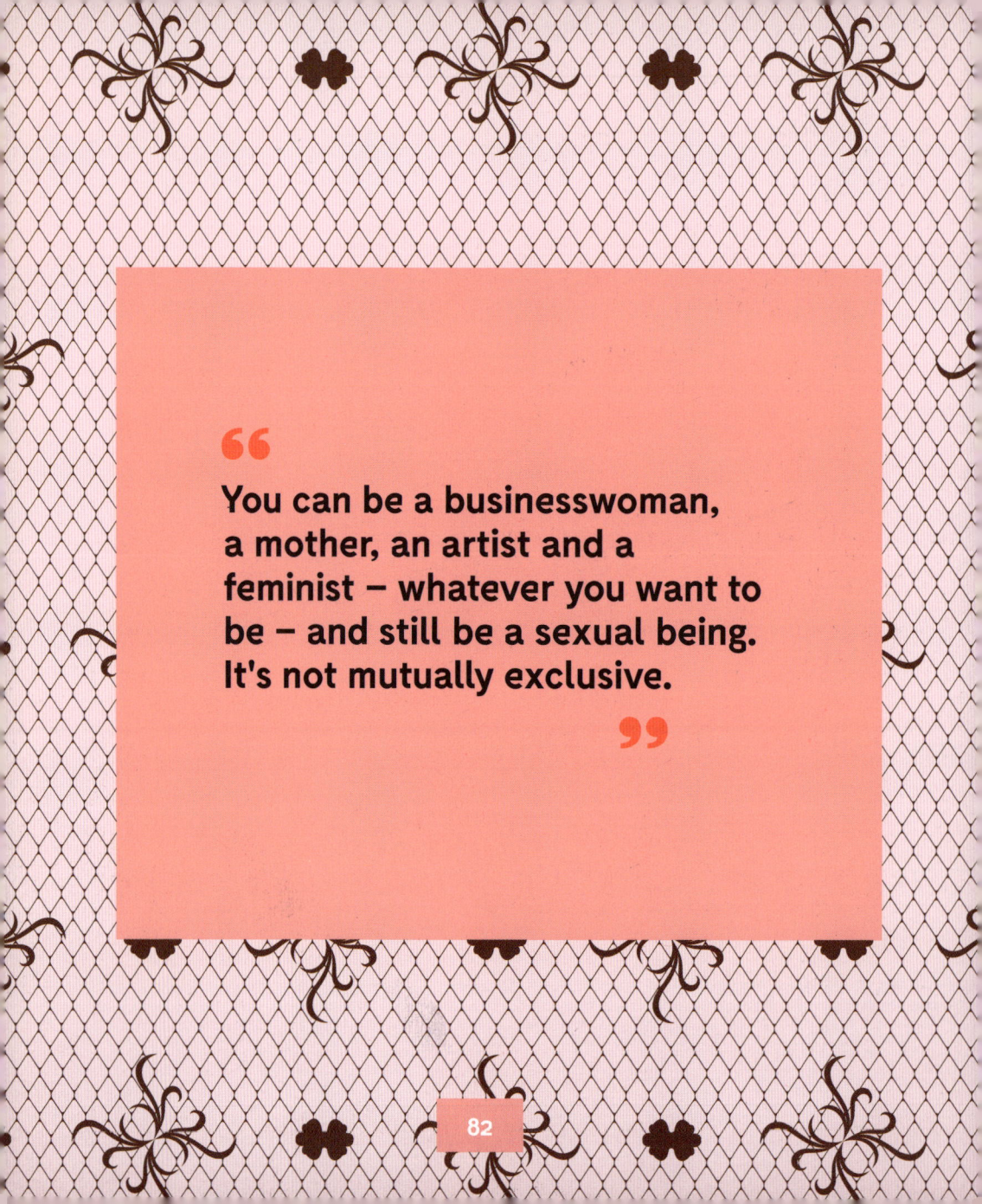

> You can be a businesswoman, a mother, an artist and a feminist – whatever you want to be – and still be a sexual being. It's not mutually exclusive.

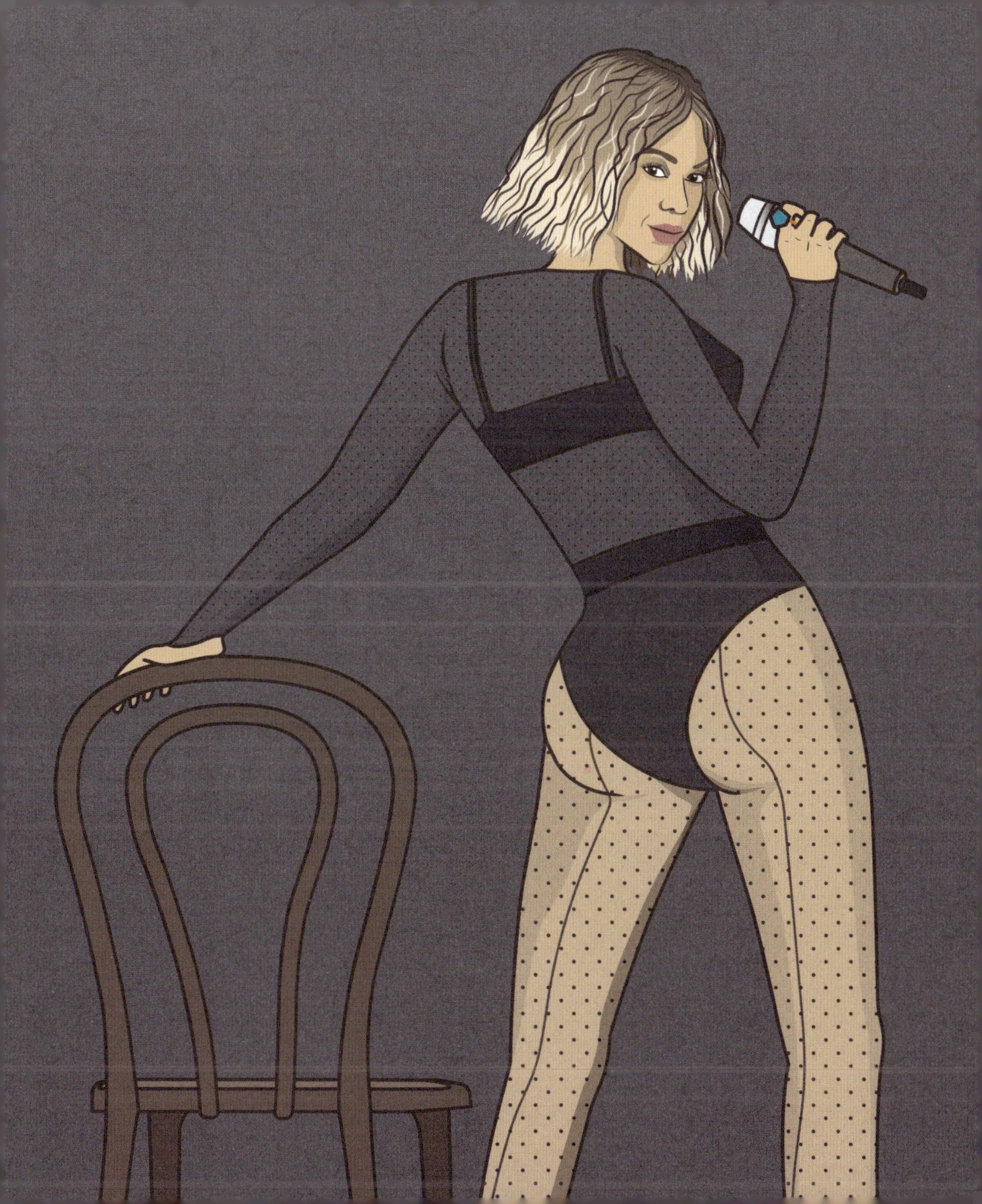

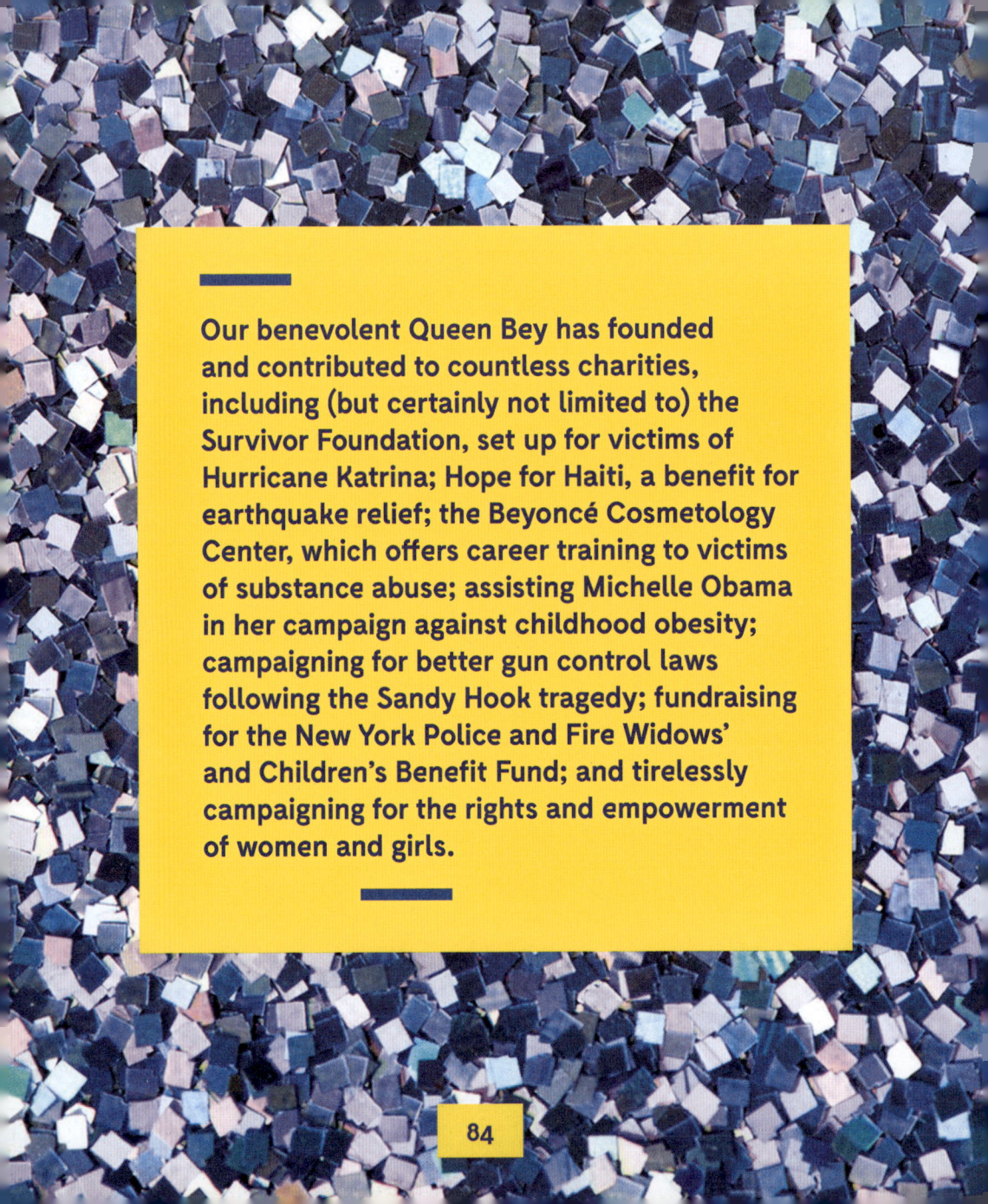

Our benevolent Queen Bey has founded and contributed to countless charities, including (but certainly not limited to) the Survivor Foundation, set up for victims of Hurricane Katrina; Hope for Haiti, a benefit for earthquake relief; the Beyoncé Cosmetology Center, which offers career training to victims of substance abuse; assisting Michelle Obama in her campaign against childhood obesity; campaigning for better gun control laws following the Sandy Hook tragedy; fundraising for the New York Police and Fire Widows' and Children's Benefit Fund; and tirelessly campaigning for the rights and empowerment of women and girls.

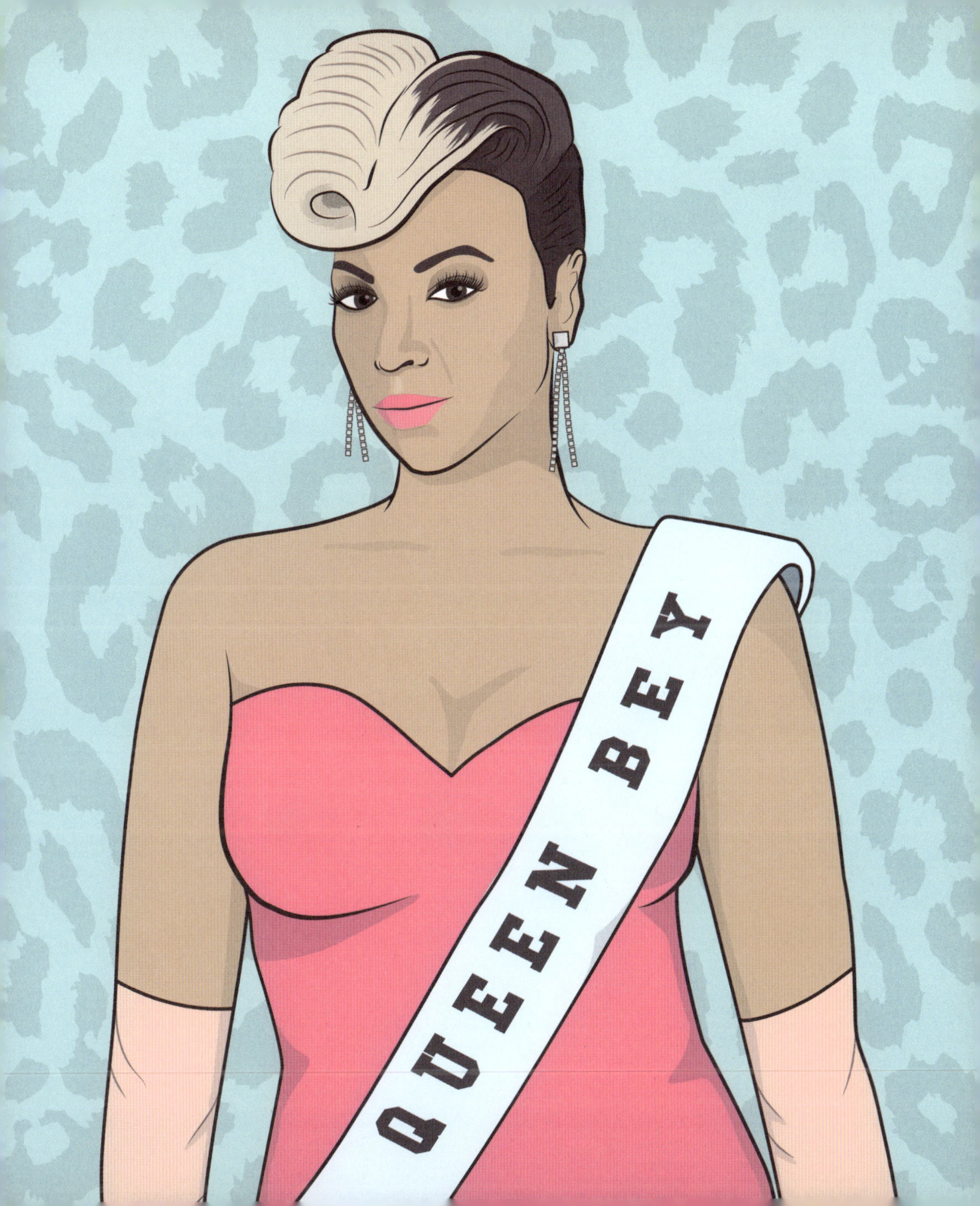
QUEEN BEY

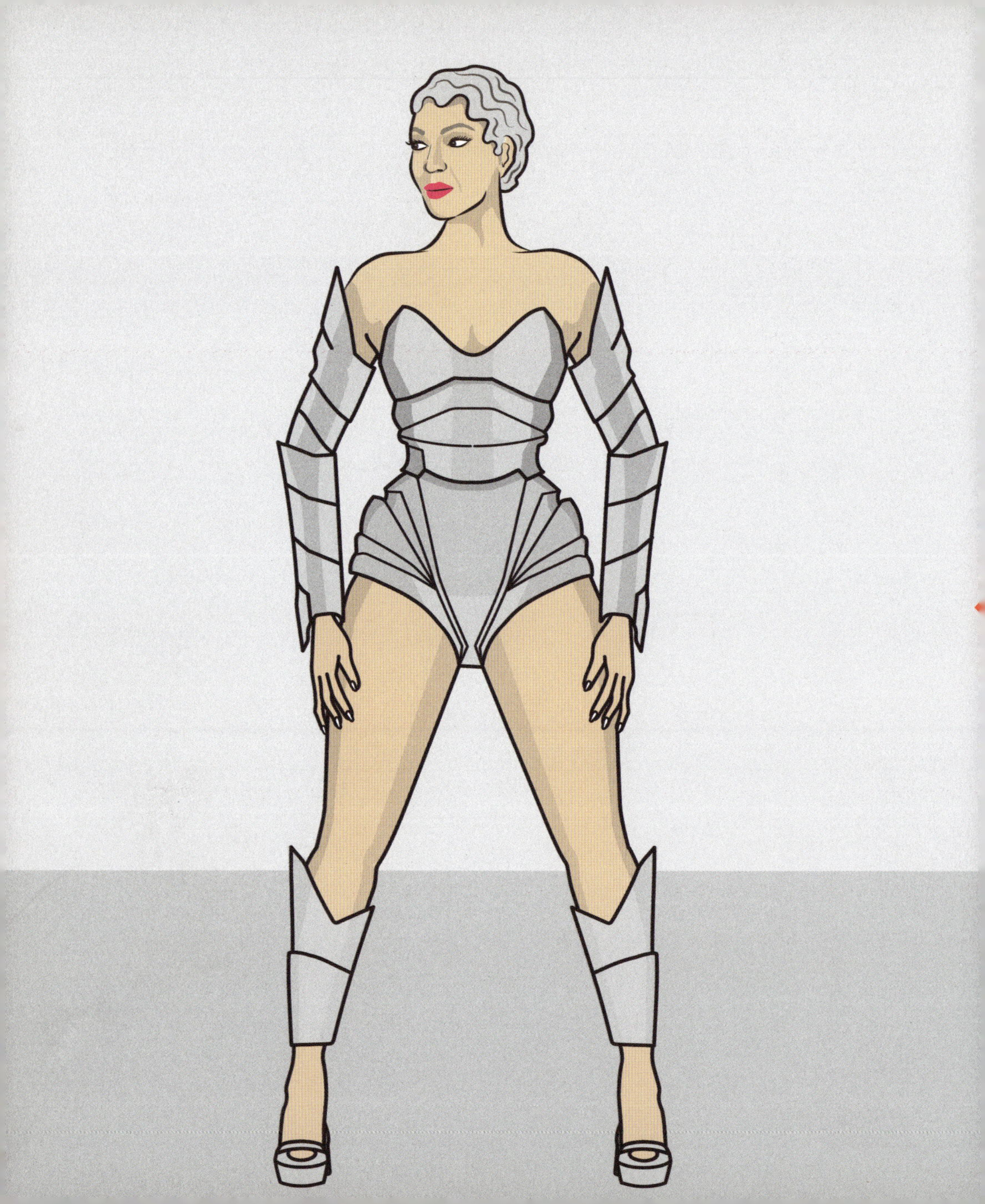

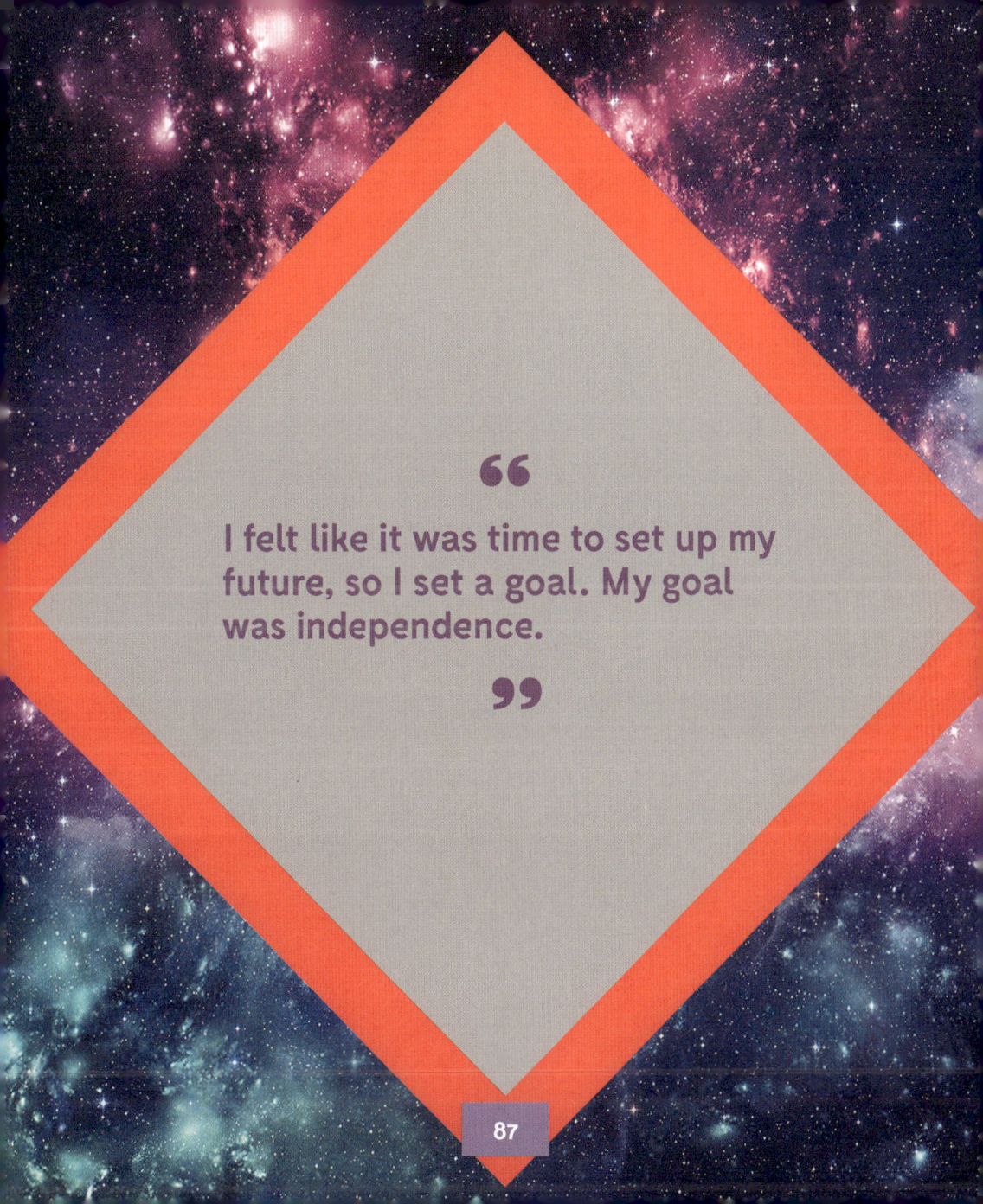

> I felt like it was time to set up my future, so I set a goal. My goal was independence.

GODI

DESS

LOVE & FAMILY

1999-2000: Beyoncé and Jay meet

2001: The pair begin to date after sharing the cover of *Vanity Fair* together

2002: '03 Bonnie & Clyde' collaboration

2003: Bey & Jay go public; 'Crazy In Love' collaboration

2004: First red carpet appearance together at the MTV VMAs

2006: Photos from the couple's trip to France documented on Bey's website

2007: Engagement announcement

2008: Beyoncé and Jay Z tie the knot in NYC!

BEYONCÉ & JAY Z 'CRAZY IN LOVE' TIMELINE

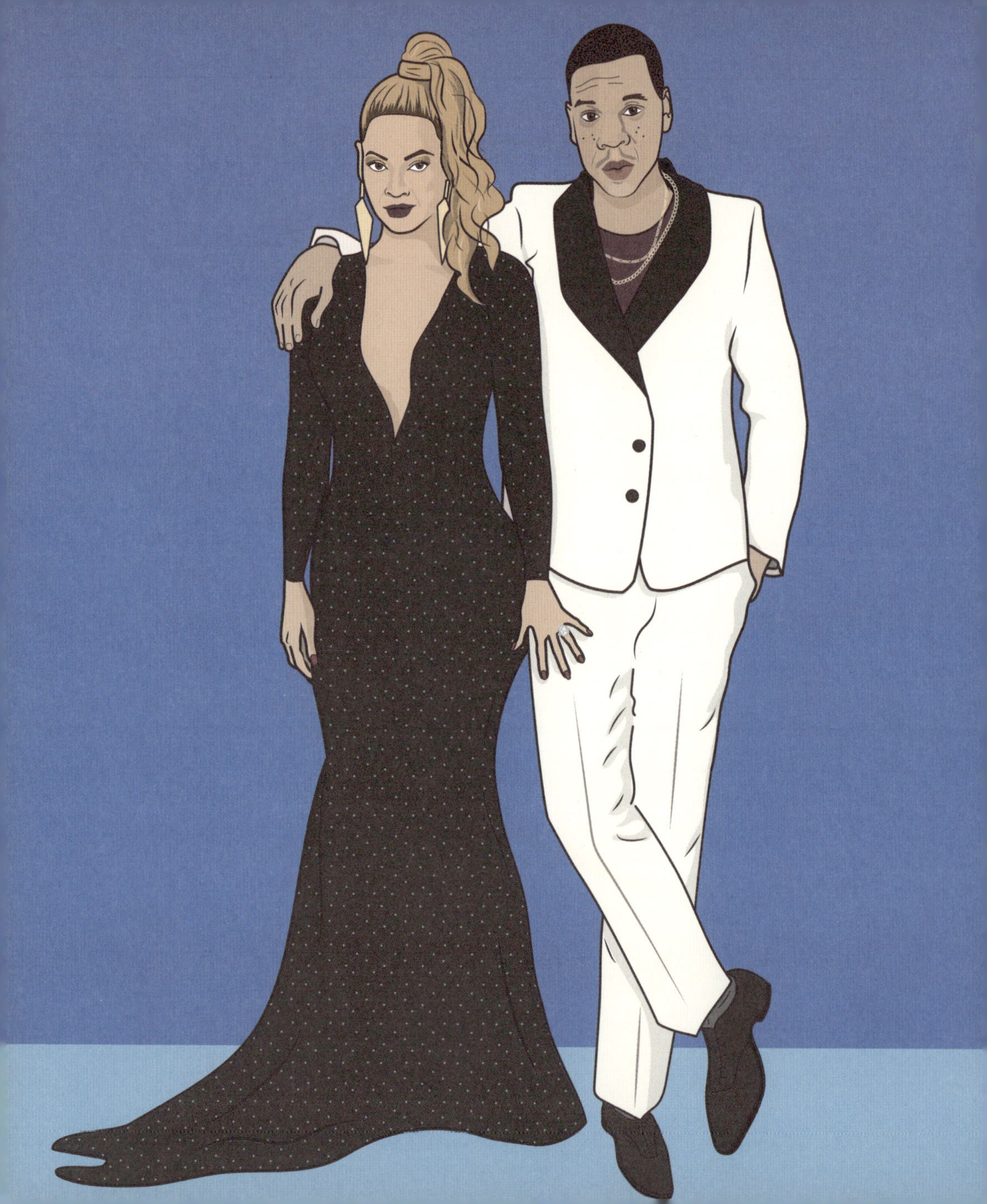

"[In 2001] we were just beginning to try to date each other. Well, you know, you've got to try first. You got to dazzle . . . wine and dine. She's a charming Southern girl, you know, she's not [easily] impressed ..."

Jay Z

Jay Z confirmed in 2013 that one of his lines – "She was a good girl 'til she knew me" – was about Beyoncé. When asked whether she's still a good girl, Jay laughed, "Nah. She's gangsta now."

In 2017, Bey and Jay's combined net worth clocked in at over $1.16 billion!

> **WE TOOK OUR TIME AND DEVELOPED AN UNBREAKABLE FRIENDSHIP BEFORE WE GOT MARRIED.**

In mid-2018, Beyoncé and Jay Z – aka The Carters – dropped their first joint album, *Everything is Love* – a conclusion to the musical conversation that began with the call of Bey's *Lemonade* in 2016 and continued with the response of Jay Z's *4:44* in 2017. Matt Miller from *Esquire* described the album as "a joyous and enlightened closing statement that acts as a finale to the greatest trilogy in modern music."

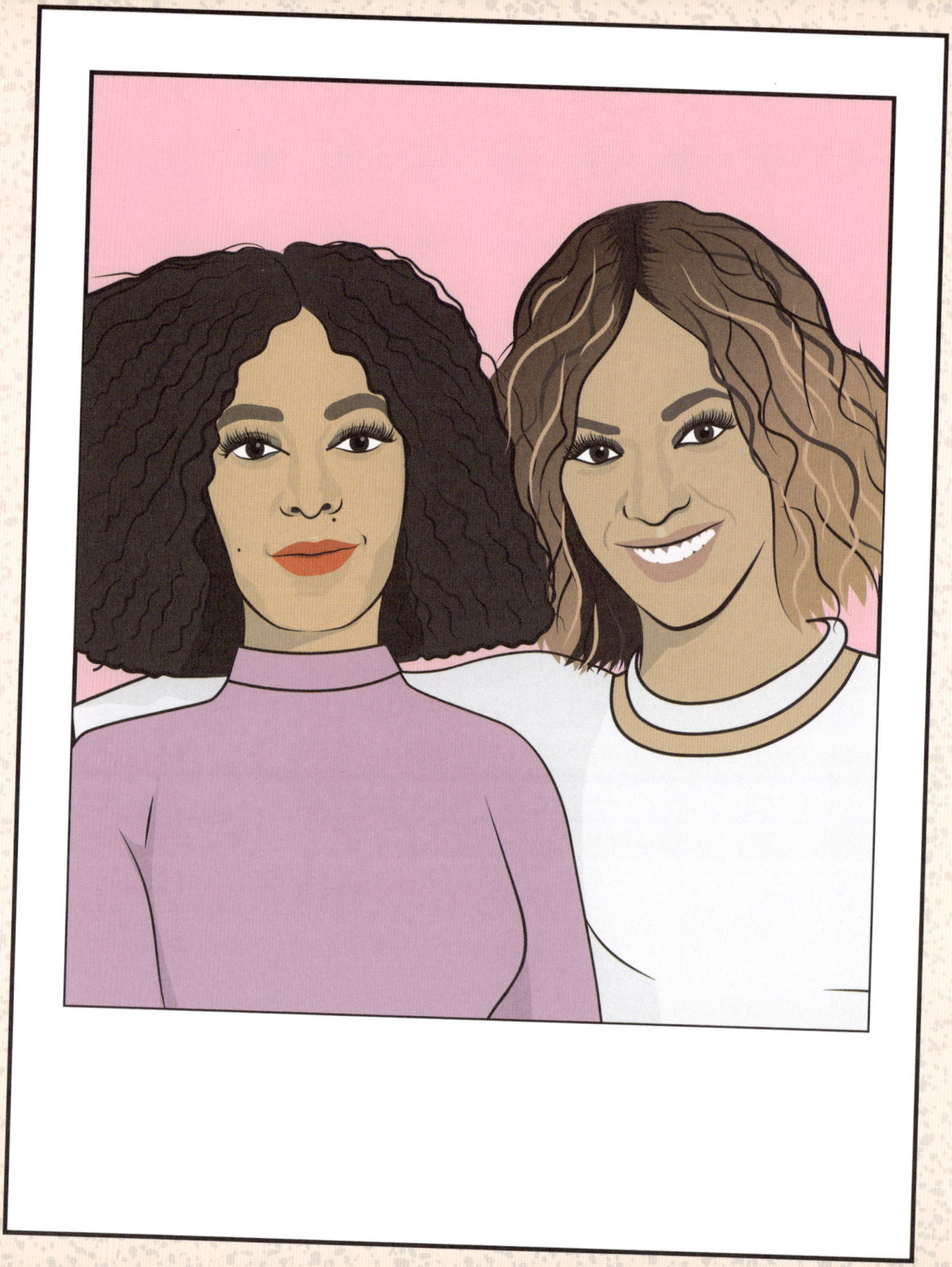

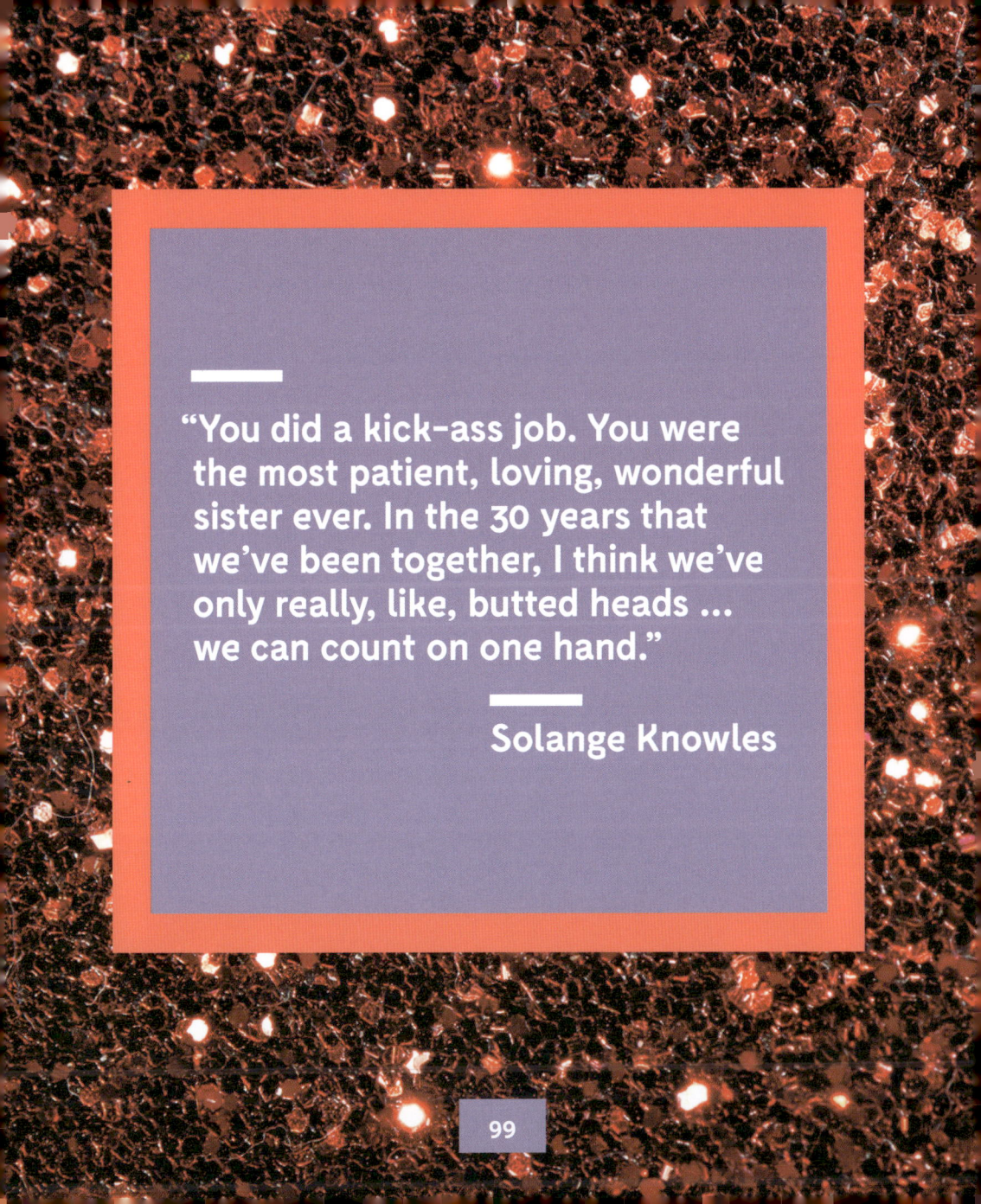

"You did a kick-ass job. You were the most patient, loving, wonderful sister ever. In the 30 years that we've been together, I think we've only really, like, butted heads … we can count on one hand."

Solange Knowles

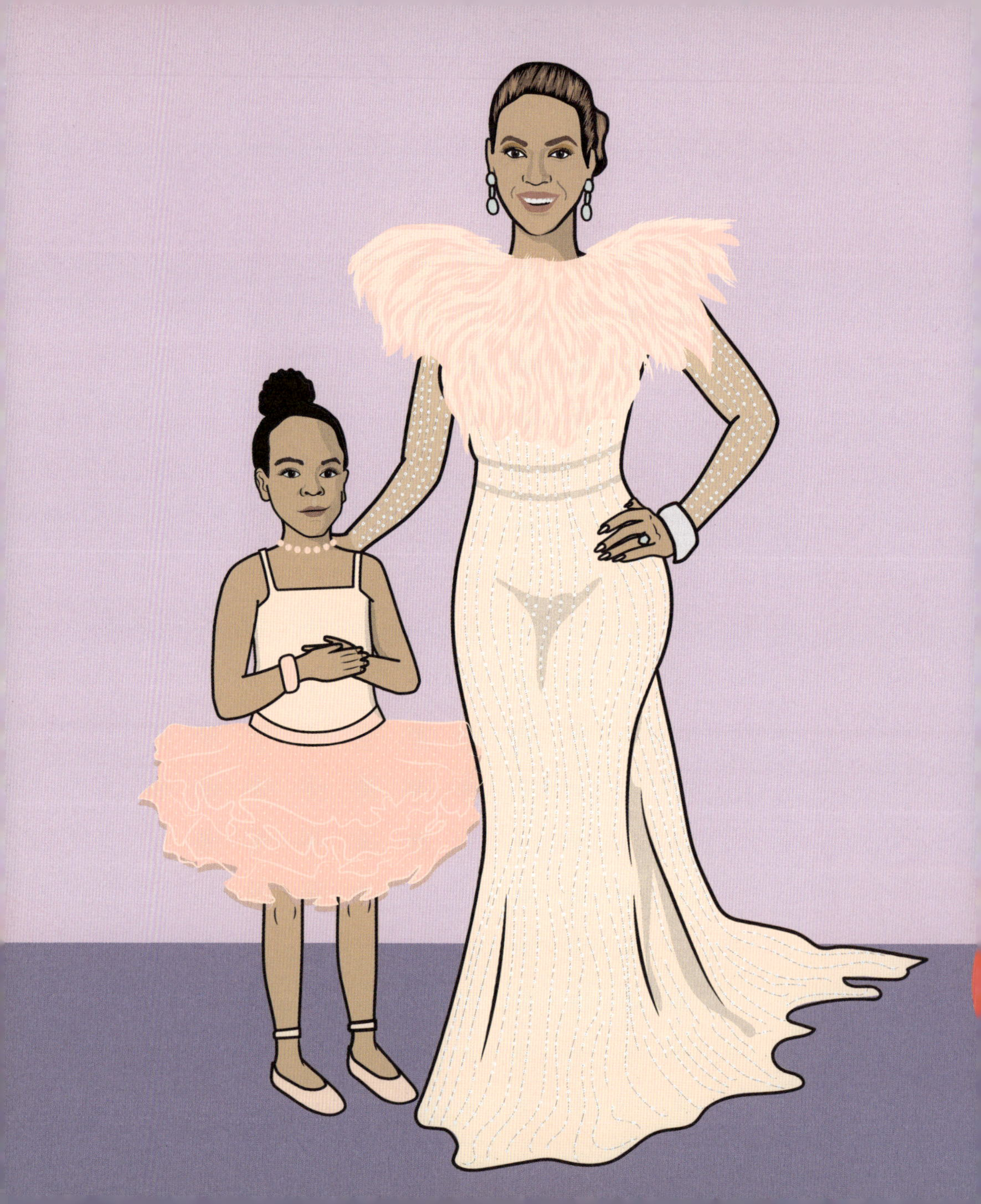

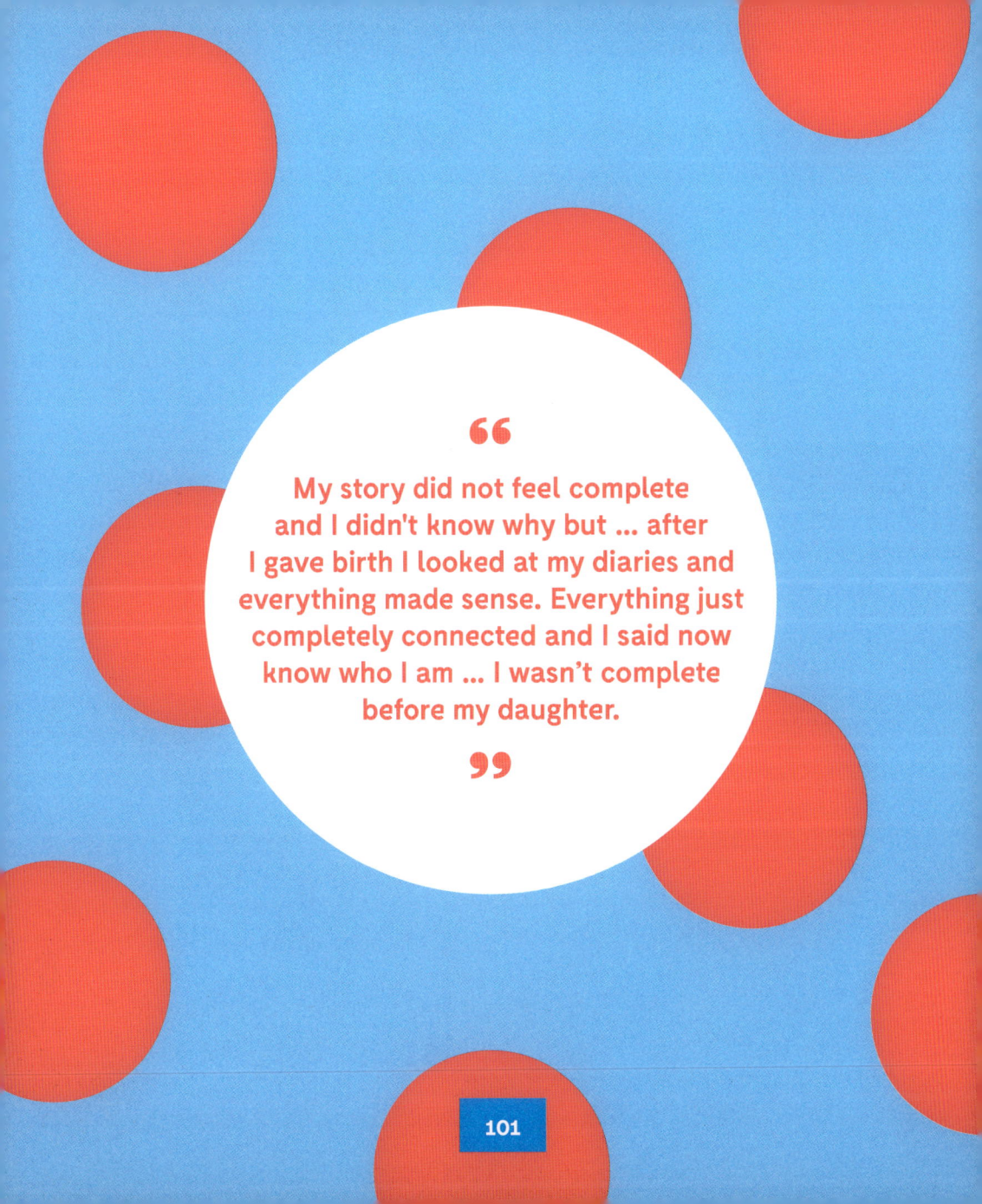

> My story did not feel complete and I didn't know why but ... after I gave birth I looked at my diaries and everything made sense. Everything just completely connected and I said now know who I am ... I wasn't complete before my daughter.

> I feel more beautiful than I've ever felt, because I've given birth. I have never felt so connected and never felt like I had such a purpose on this earth.

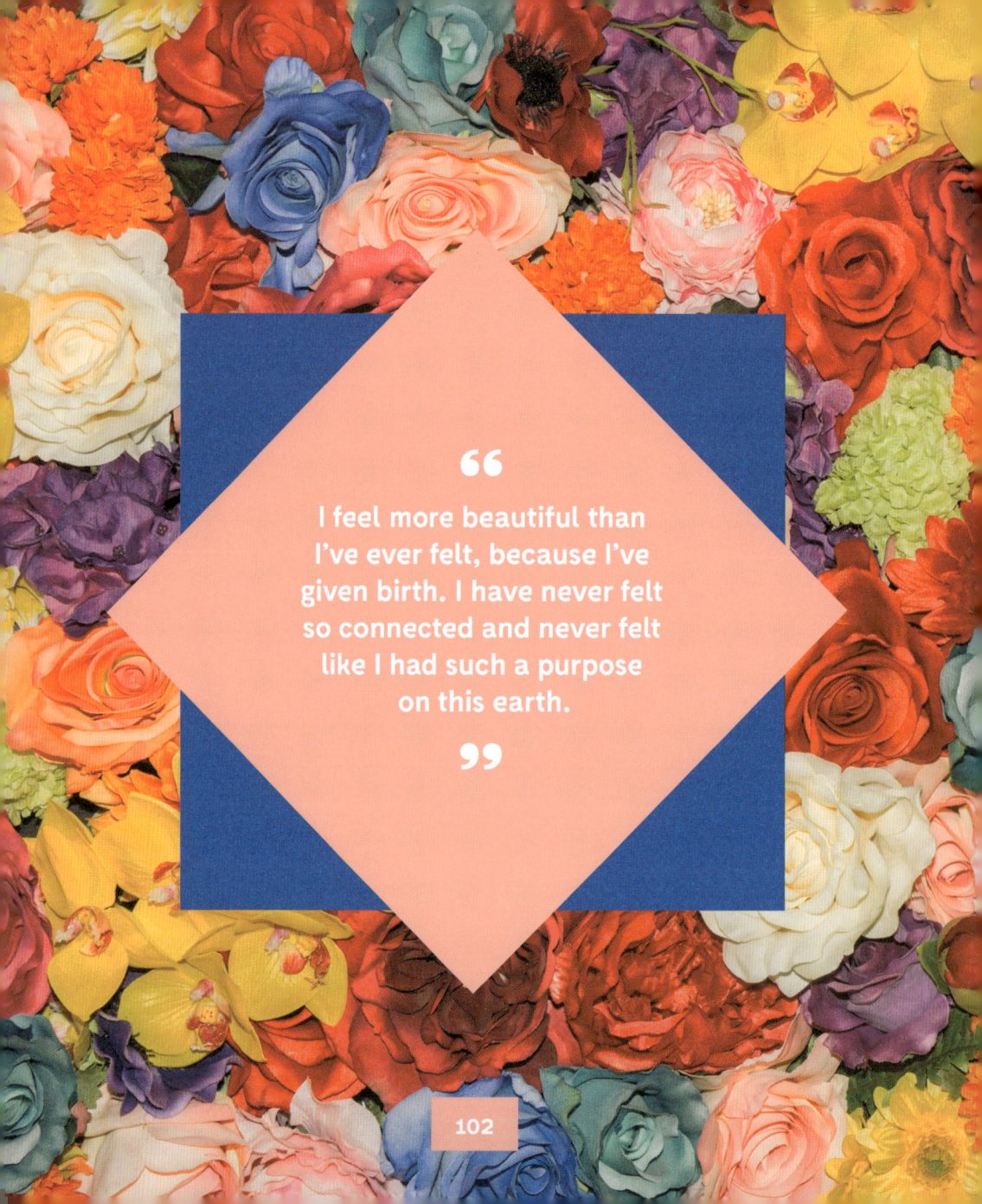

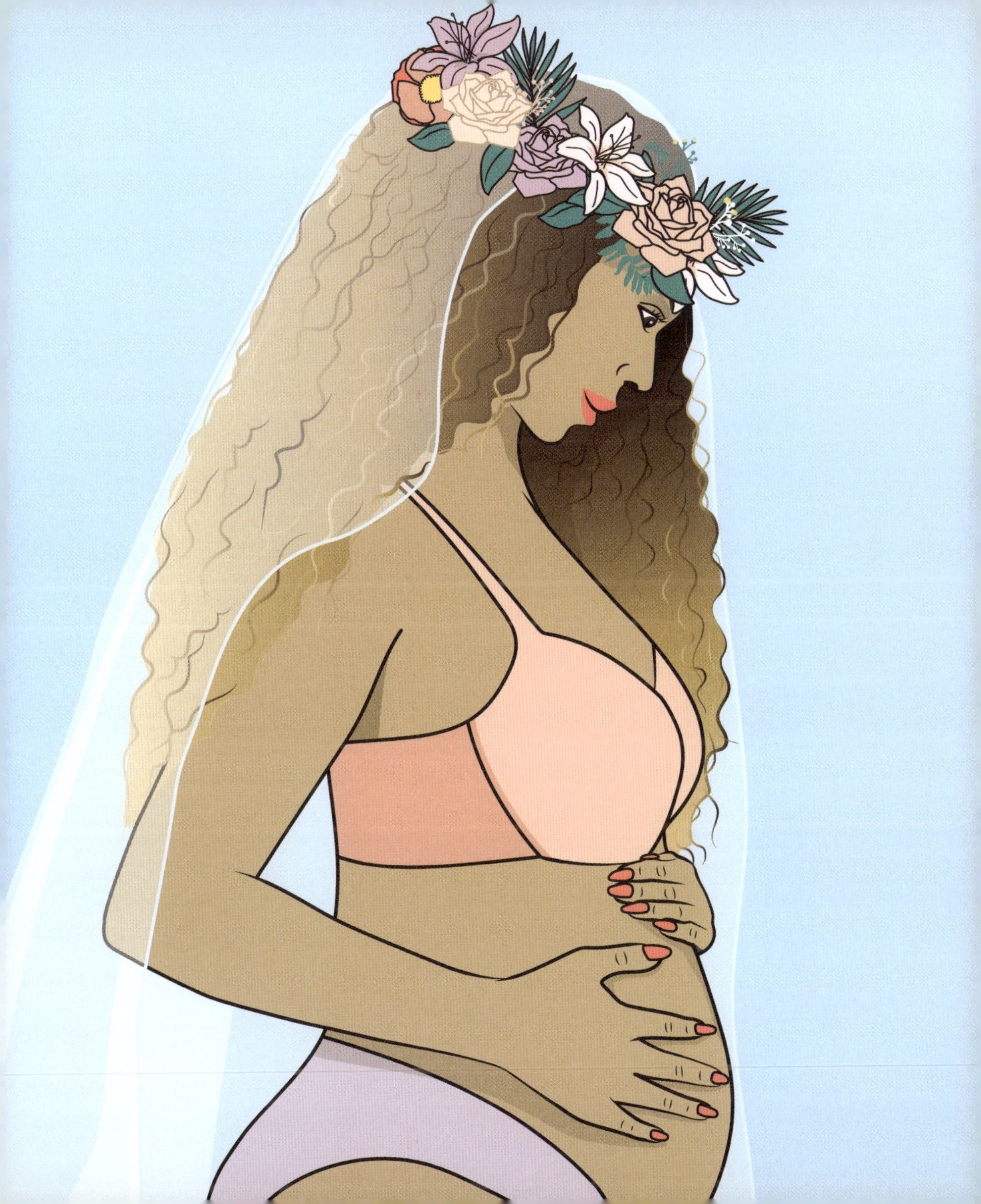

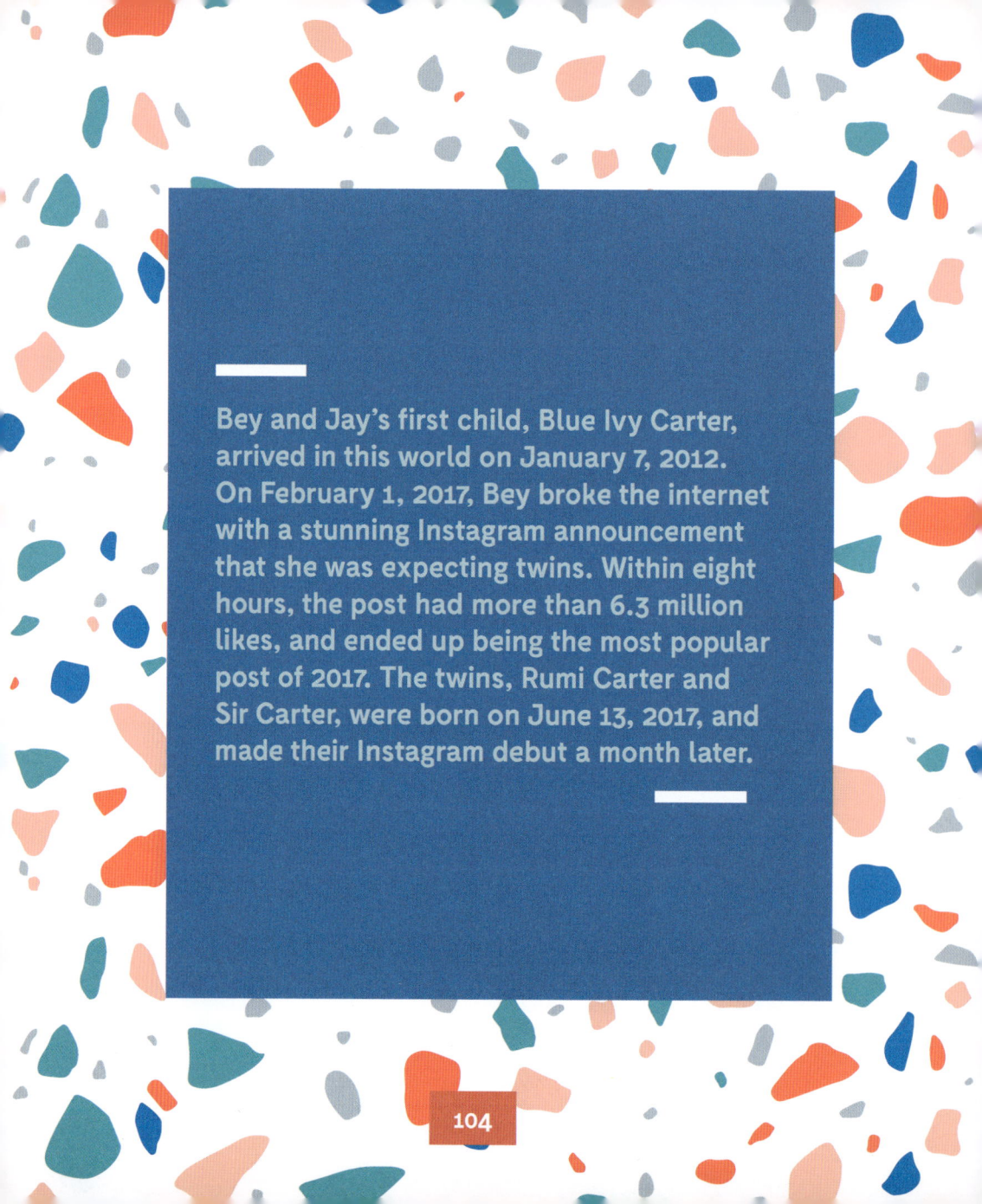

—

Bey and Jay's first child, Blue Ivy Carter, arrived in this world on January 7, 2012. On February 1, 2017, Bey broke the internet with a stunning Instagram announcement that she was expecting twins. Within eight hours, the post had more than 6.3 million likes, and ended up being the most popular post of 2017. The twins, Rumi Carter and Sir Carter, were born on June 13, 2017, and made their Instagram debut a month later.

—

At just two days old, Blue Ivy became the youngest person to ever appear on the Billboard 100 chart after her cries and heartbeat appeared on papa Jay Z's track 'Glory' in 2012.

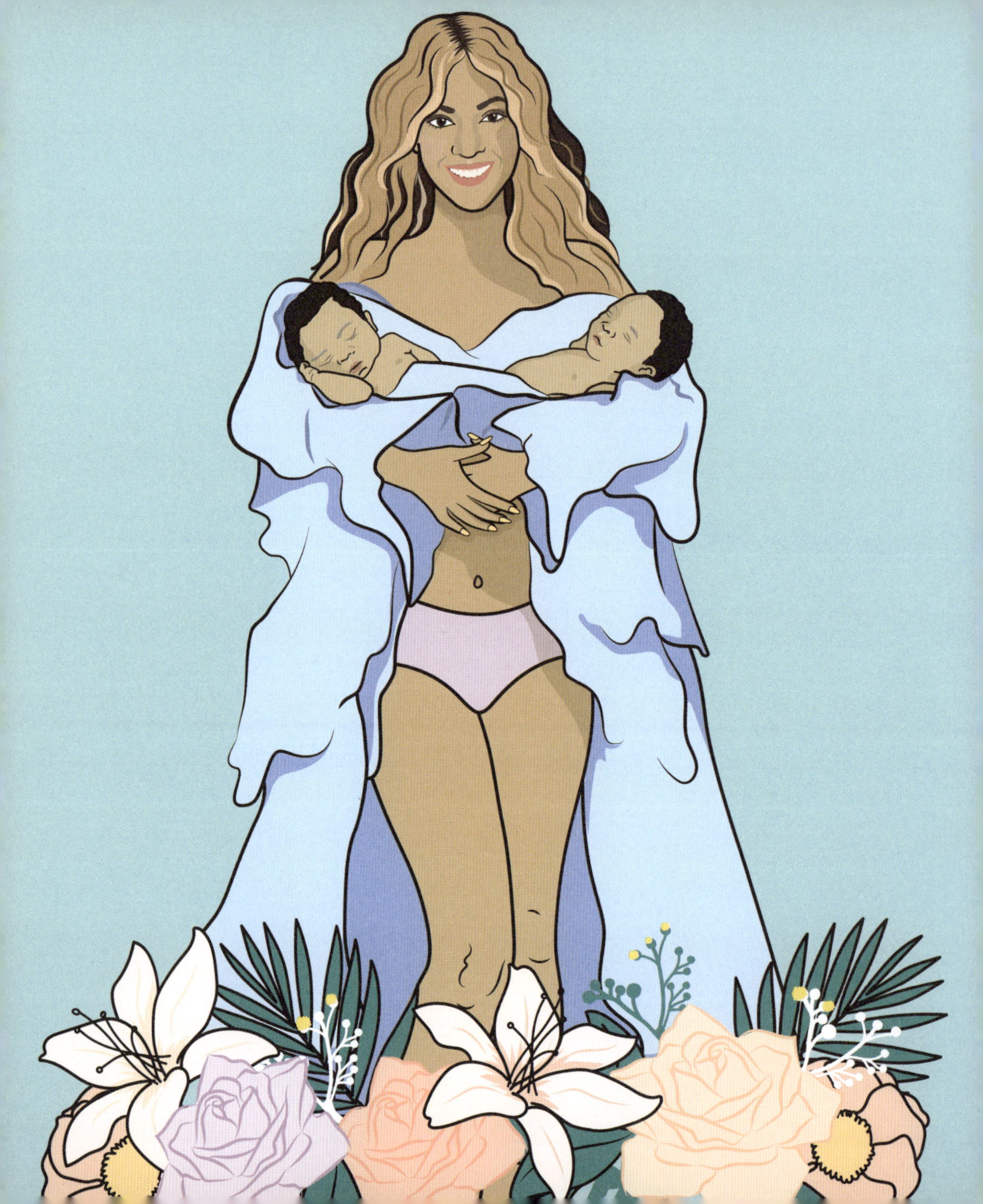

> Right now, after giving birth, I really understand the power of my body, I just feel my body means something completely different. I feel a lot more confident about it ... Even being heavier, thinner, whatever. I feel a lot more like a woman. More feminine, more sensual. And no shame.

> **DO ONE THING FOR ANOTHER HUMAN BEING, NOTHING IS TOO SMALL. IT BEGINS WITH EACH OF US.**
>
> **MAKE YOUR MARK AND SAY 'I WAS HERE'.**